SPIRIT AND
SACRAMENT

Spirit and Sacrament

THE HUMANIZING
EXPERIENCE

by Joseph M. Powers

A Continuum Book
The Seabury Press · New York

The Seabury Press, Inc.
815 Second Avenue
New York, N.Y. 10017

Library of Congress Catalog Card Number: 72-10566
ISBN: 0-8164-1121-2

For J. and James
Richard and D.
David, Joni and John V.

By reason of his union with Christ, the source of life, man attains to a new fulfillment of himself, to a transcendent humanism which gives him his greatest possible perfection: this is the highest goal of personal achievement.

POPE PAUL VI
Populorum Progressio
(n.16)

Contents

Preface

These reflections have been written in a search for meaning which is as honest as their author can make them. The problem of meaning is the constant religious and theological problem. As we confront our own experience, we find within ourselves the need to integrate and unify it in some coherent way. Without this process of integration we would live in a world devoid of meaning. We have a symbol for that kind of life: hell, life lived in fragmentation and alienation. And it is out of this kind of need that we create the symbol systems which gather our experience into a manageable coherence. Structure, law, ritual, language—all of these symbolic realities give our lives the unity which they must have.

But there is something about a symbol system which resists the broader matrix of cultural development and change within which the symbol system lives. Maybe it is because they perform such a profound and critical function in our lives, but whatever the reason, we tend to canonize, to sacralize them. And so they take on their own sacred life and, like the children of Israel, we fear to touch or tamper with them lest we die. But human history, human culture go on, change, develop. And it always happens that the gap between the experience which should be contained in or facilitated by our symbol systems and the broader cultural experience within which we live becomes so

great that someone must eventually ask, "What does it mean?"
What does "God" mean? What does this social structure
mean? What do these laws mean? What does this ritual mean?

It is beyond triteness to say that we live in a time of change,
a time when the problem of meaning is particularly critical. We
hear the question asked from every side, addressed to almost
every symbol system. In some instances, the question implies
the meaninglessness of the symbols which structure our life, our
experience and the urge to tear the whole thing down. These
reflections are not made in that spirit. Rather, they are an
attempt to discover what experience—human experience—
these symbols should contain and produce. They are written in
an attempt to find how we might reload these symbols with the
power they should have for our lives.

It should be of some comfort to realize that this is not the
first such period in the life of the Church. The beard-pulling,
the armies of sailors and gladiators which marked the development of doctrine from its New Testament expression to that of
Nicaea and Chalcedon, the condemnation of Aquinas' use of
the pagan Aristotle—these struggles should indicate to us that,
in spite of all the difficulty, we can survive these periods of
change and conflict. But what is most critical in these times is
our own courage to ask the question of meaning honestly and
openly. To question is not to reject. It is rather the attempt to
find out what the symbols meant in the first place and what
they should be saying to our lives here and now. Only a strong
and courageous faith can ask this question in the hope that it
will emerge stronger and firmer than before.

It is the hope of this author that these reflections will be
of some assistance in the renewal within our own lives which
the Spirit of the Lord can bring about and for which these
times cry out.

SPIRIT AND
SACRAMENT

God

Among the stories in the book of Exodus connected with the Sinai experience, the Jahwist, with his typical reserve in the face of the mystery of God, tells a story about Moses which makes a profound statement about both God and man. Climbing down from Horeb, the mountain of the covenant, Moses is astounded to find the people "playing" around the golden calf which Aaron had sculpted for them. Moses' anger flares; the tablets of the covenant, engraved by God's own hand, fly from his hands and shatter against the foot of the mountain. The sons of Levi are ordained in a blood bath; a plague sweeps through the people to purge them from their guilt. But the faithfulness of the Lord overcomes His anger and He summons Moses to lead the people forward into the land of the promise. But the Lord refuses to go along with the people lest His holiness consume them. Moses is shaken at this. He pleads with the Lord. The absence of the Lord discredits Moses' leadership and threatens the very possibility of the fulfillment of the promise. So, because of His love for Moses and because of Moses' plea, the Lord relents; "This very thing which we have spoken, I will do; for you have found favor in my sight and I know you by name." (33:17)

Suddenly, something stirs inside Moses. He blurts out, "I pray you, show me your glory!" Patiently, the Lord answers, "I will make all my goodness pass before you, and I will proclaim before you my name, 'the Lord,' . . . but you cannot see my face, for man cannot see me and live." (33:19–20) But the Lord does grant Moses a favor. He orders Moses to stand on a nearby rock and says, ". . . while my glory passes by you, I will put you in a cleft of the rock and I will cover you with my hand until I have passed by; then I will take away my hand and you shall see my back but my face shall not be seen." (33:22–23) And the majesty of the Lord passes before Moses as the Lord proclaims, "The Lord! The Lord! A God merciful and gracious, slow to anger and abounding in steadfast love and faithfulness . . ." (34:6) Moses fall to his face and worships the Lord, praying that the Lord will go with His people, that He will forgive their sin, that He will take the people for His inheritance.

The narrative ends there, as if the editor would suggest that the answer to Moses' prayer constitutes the rest of the Old Testament history. But the plea which Moses blurted out at the foot of Horeb goes on, "Show me your face!" For in that plea there is contained the yearning and searching which forms the specifically *religious* dimension of human existence. Delighted, enraptured or frightened and threatened by the very depths of his own existence, man reaches out to something beyond his own limits to serve at once as the anchor and the magnet of his being. And since the time of E. Le Roy, philosophers and theologians have labeled this search "The Problem of God."

The Problem

Of course, God is not a problem for everyone. Some simply settle for life as it strikes us without the complication which a deeper principle of understanding and judgment introduce into a world already sufficiently complicated. At the opposite end of the human spectrum, others settle for the "God of the fathers," accepting without question the God given to them by a cultural or religious spirit who is sufficient justification for existence amid slings and sorrows. But our concern here is for those of us who sit, like Linus, in our pumpkin patch every Halloween (or any other time) screaming "Show yourself!" And our anxiety is that, like the Great Pumpkin, the One we long to see never shows up. So we either give up the search, like the vultures which circle around rumored carrion, or adopt Linus' posture in the face of Lucy's "hard-headed realism," "Wait till next year!"

The reason why God is a "problem" for us is perhaps the reason why anything is a problem. A problem is simply someone or something whose reality or intelligibility is not apparent or is incongruous from the evidence or experience at hand. Problems force us to deepen or expand the focus of our attention and thus integrate this new and problematic reality into our general understanding of ourselves and our world. Problems are a "shock," which call our attention to another "province" of reality which lies beyond the things to which we habitually "pay attention." And the deepening or expanding of consciousness involved in the "solution" of our "problem" gives us a correspondingly deeper or broader vision of ourselves and our world, a self and a world richer as seer and seen. This may or may not have immediate implications for the conduct of our lives or for the techniques of our science, but at its base, the "solution" is more properly an integration of our being and vision in our world. In this light, the "problem of God" is basically a problem of man—the problem of our being in our world, the problem of "managing" our existence, the problem of the justification of our and the world's existence and shape.

The problem keeps changing shape. Not too long ago, we could say, "I believe in God." People would agree or disagree. They would either say that they believed in God or that they didn't believe in God. And people more or less knew what they meant when they talked about it. Whether it was "my God" or "your God," there was at least a general cultural acceptance of the content of the language we used. But today, the increasingly general reaction we face when we even use the word is a puzzled look. "God? I can follow everything you say except for that word 'God.' " And it's not that people have suddenly taken leave of their senses. Rather they (and we!) have come to live in a world where the older image and function of God have "died." In an older and more "primitive" culture (far from "dead" even today) there were definite things for God to do, definite kinds of action in which His presence could be clearly apparent. Historically, "God" has been used as the explanation for everything over which man seemed to have no control. He was variously praised or blessed for what we could not explain or control. If we can't explain it, "God knows!" If the rain made the crops and flowers grow, we were grateful to God; if it rained too much and dams broke and cities and farms flooded out, we still looked for an "act of God" clause in our insurance policy. A perusal of the "Orationes diversae" section of the *Missale Romanum* shows at once the depth of our trust in God and the optimism of our estimations of His prowess. War, peace, sickness, health, chastity, tears—they are all His doing. An inspection of the blessings by which the works of man were placed in God's keeping covers quite a field—plants, beer, fire engines, the marriage bed and, in case something should be produced by man's ingenuity which the blessings do not quite cover, a *benedictio ad omnia,* a blessing so worded that it fits everything. And not too long ago a German pointed out the difference between Germans and Americans with the words, "We Germans write *'Gott mit uns'* on our swords and you Americans write 'In God we trust' on your money."

But things have changed. If we can't explain something, we tend to wait a while. Someone will come up with an answer if the problem becomes pressing enough. We may not be able to stop hurricanes, but we can see them coming for days and weeks before they strike and protect ourselves. And we can make it rain, in some circumstances. Sickness and health are medical rather than religious problems, war and peace are political problems, chastity and tears could well be psychological problems—all of which can be handled by the appropriate scientists or technicians. And philosophers of science would close out any possibility of a "god of the natural gaps" by saying that nature is not only "queerer than we think," but that it is "queerer than we could ever imagine."

No wonder, then, that we meet with puzzled looks when we speak of "God." The enormous strides we have made in the understanding and manipulation of nature have left less and less for God to do. And, as has been waggishly pointed out, "God has died, not from overwork but from boredom." So something comforting, something justifying from our past is, if not entirely gone, at least present in the consciousness of fewer and fewer people. And is there not a poignancy for ourselves in the remark so facetiously attributed to Harry Truman, "I didn't know Him personally, but I hear that He was a damn fine person."

So "God" becomes a problem for us. What was once relatively clear (they always told us God was a mystery) is now quite unclear for us. Are we wrong? Are the Lucies of the world right after all? We have a number of options.

We can go back to the specifically "religious" sources of knowledge and understanding to root our conviction in the experience of those who "saw God." But, if we take the trouble to look at what is there, there is little comfort in store for us. We see Moses staring at the hindmost parts of God in the Elohist saga. In the saga of the Jahwist, Moses asked for God's name and received a promise, "I will be there." Jacob had a wrestling match with——? (Gen 32:22–32) In terms of the meaning of our religious language, the descriptions of Ezekiel (1:4 ff.) and Daniel might elicit a response something like, "Like wow! man, like what was he dropping?" And, as if this were not discouraging enough, we come eventually to the crushingly final judgment of John, "No one has ever seen God!" (1:18, I Jn 4:12)

This discouragement is not alleviated when we look to those who "saw God" in mysticism. Juliana of Norwich and John of the Cross speak of their knowledge as an "entrance into un-knowing" and John described the object of his search and his finding simply as "I-don't-know what" (*no sé qué*). And if their language is not so frankly negative, the mystics stumble and stammer in an attempt to give us some idea of the One for whom they search and whom they encounter in some way.

It does no good, then, to pretend that we are better or less worldly than those who ask for some idea of what we mean by "God." There is nothing we can point to in our experience or theirs which is "God." There is only absence.

The absence of God can be a terrible crisis for sacramental religion. This is particularly the case when sacramental religion promises to "deliver" God to the believer. This is a temptation for religion in every age. Our culturally conditioned "concept of God" lays claim all too easily to an "objectivity" which ignores the transcendent difference of God, and we fashion idols for ourselves. Sacred law, sacred order, sacred institutions, sacred times, sacred places, obvious human achievements and institutions, take on an eternal, other-worldly character. We forget that like the idols of the Gentiles, these are really the work of man's hands. But fortunately time does march on and history has a way of unmasking our pretensions. One generation has a way of uncanonizing what an earlier generation elevated to the level of the sacred.

Thus again and again we are forced back to the question of the reality and meaning of "God." Obviously the answer cannot be something we can point to and say, "There. That's God." If this were true, there would be no "problem of God." At least someone, somewhere could simply point to the reality and it would be there to be seen. But this is precisely what we cannot do. The reality of what we mean by "God" is not the "object" of any experience, ordinary or extraordinary. However, if our talk about and belief in God is to be realistic at all, it must somehow refer to our experience. Otherwise, our language is simply meaningless. So we are caught in a dilemma when we come to speak of God. On the one hand, there is no object within our experience which we can call "God" (unless it be an idol of our own fashioning) and, on the other hand, our language must have some experiential referent if it is to have meaning.

This has something to say to us about the "absence" of God which has been the theme of our initial meditation. Absence, the lack of a certain spatial or personal presence happens in at least two different ways. It happens when the reality whose presence I seek is simply not where I expect to find it. The coffee pot is either "there" or it is "not there." My experience falls on *nothing*. But there is also an absence in which the reality I search for eludes me because it is "disguised." I may expect the coffee pot to be a stainless-steel electric percolator. I look in the cupboard and don't see a stainless-steel electric percolator. So there is no coffee pot there, as far as I can see. The fact may well be that there is a fine glass filter carafe which is, in fact, a coffee pot. So the coffee pot *is* there, but the coffee pot I expect to find is *not* there. Fugitives take advantage of this kind of human expectation to avoid capture.

The "absence of God" is the second kind of absence. It is a contradiction of our understandable human desire to "see God," to be able to point to the ultimate reality as a secure object within the field of some kind of perception. But, as has been said, this is precisely what we cannot do with God. And our search ends with an experience of "nothing." We are like the vultures Merton alludes to, birds of appetite who hover over a place where the object of desire is supposed to be. But they look for the wrong thing and cannot see what really is there. So they fly away as their interest wanes and disappears.

What then do we mean by God and how do we come to know of the reality of God? Stated briefly, "God" is the ultimate answer to the ultimate question which our existence is. "God" is the "yes" of existence and belief in God is possible to the extent that we experience the "yes" as the answer to our own ultimate question, our very existence. Thus, our understanding of the meaning and reality of God comes down to our understanding of a question, an answer and an experience which discloses this answer. In this analysis we are engaged in what is called a "theodicy," a justification of God's meaning and reality in terms of human experience. But instead of a cosmological or ethical theodicy, this theodicy will try to operate more in terms of human experience, a more experiential or even "mystical" theodicy.

The question we are asked is Tillich's question of "ultimate concern." However, we want to go behind this formulation to find the *experience* which raises this question. The reason for this is, as we have seen, that any language which goes beyond the province of what we define and "pay attention to" as "ordinary experience" immediately raises the question of meaning, and the question here is not one of an abstract relation of concept to object but the more concrete question of whether this language refers to and communicates a real human experience. Thus, our question, the "God-question," comes down to this, is there an experience which asks us the radical, ultimate fundamental question? Does our experience ever drive us to ask Hamlet's question, "To be or not to be?" Our contention here is that there is such an experience and that "God" is one answer to the question which this experience raises.

Of course, we should be aware of the fact that the "radical," the "fundamental," the "ultimate" are very relative terms, relative to the ways in which one defines reality. One tends to define one's ultimate in terms of the scope which one permits one's world to possess. Thus, if, for example, the "real world" is the world of one's intense social or political activity, one tends to see everything and to measure its reality in terms of this primary province of attention. Whatever is not somehow involved in this confine of attention and action is "unreal," "irrelevant." This is the "real world." Such a person eventually runs up against a "shock" in his life. Something is wrong; he can't cope with himself or his world, he finds himself counter-productive even in terms of the goals and reality he sets for himself and society. This shock forces a man to question his going definition of the real and opens up for him another "world," a world which "transcends" what he has defined as the "real world." At a deeper level, but pervading the whole "real world," he finds a deeper reality which he must incorporate into his understanding and interpretation of his experience. Or perhaps the simple process of time forces him to define his world, himself, his goals in terms of a more inclusive definition of the real. Whatever the reason, he is forced in some way to "transcend" a reality and himself within that reality because he has seen himself defining the world in terms too narrow or too shallow to explain what is revealed to him in new experience. In this sense, the "transcendent" and the "absolute" are relative indeed, relative to the person who does the transcending and who defines and justifies himself and his world in terms of "absolutes."

In this sense, then, everyone "believes in God." Everyone has some thematized or unthematized absolute in terms of which one justifies one's self and one's world. Be it power, money, respect, human goodness or something else, a "God" serves as the deepest available intellectual and ethical background for understanding and action. And this God is known in the transcendent experience of facing the deepest available experience of one's own freedom. The name of this God will vary from person to person, but it is interesting to note that in the last analysis both St. Paul and Jean-Paul Sartre insist that it requires "bad faith" not to "know God."

However, it is not in reference to these "gods" that Christian tradition speaks of "God." Indeed, the monotheism of both Israel and Christianity is a stern rejection of precisely this kind of projection of the powers of nature (earth, sky, seasons) or personal structure (aggression, sex). Indeed, if we want to identify God in terms of our needs or expectations, we would do well to keep in mind John of the Cross' sketch of the ascent of Mount Carmel in which each step is precisely a step of the negation of human desire: *nada . . . nada . . . nada . . . aún en el monte, nada!* (Nothing . . . nothing . . . nothing . . . even on the mountain, nothing!) It is interesting to note that E. Schillebeeckx, speaking of the need for a new image of God, remarks that the tradition in Christian mysticism called the "dark night of the soul" will once again become a new field of experience.

What is it, then, which forms the most central reality of our sacramental worship, the core of our reality as Church and as individuals within the Church? From what has been seen up to this point, it should be clear that it is nothing. If we go up the mountain with Elijah or with John of the Cross we never find what we seek. Elijah heard a soft wind in which it became clear to him that he was, in effect, fired. John contradicts every material and spiritual expectation with the repeated denial *ni eso . . . ni eso . . . ni eso* (not that . . . not that . . . not that).

L. Gilkey has elaborated areas of human experience in which we are radically, ultimately questioned. A number of aspects of our human experience question not merely one or another aspect of our existence as living active persons but the *whole* of ourselves. Thus, the experience of our own contingency, the fact that we cannot fashion a secure base for our lives and that all of it can crumble to dust in our very hands, that our joys and our sorrows "happen" in such unpredictable and uncontrollable ways—this experience asks us what possible base for security can there be in our lives. And the question is not theoretical. It asks us, "Why be? Why act? Why live? Why love?" Why, in a word, continue being or trying to be all that a human being means being? Again, the experience of our relativity, the fact that the meanings in terms of which we justify our own existence as worthwhile collapse and leave us threatened by facing a life devoid of any of the meanings on which we counted—this experience asks us what possible base for meaning can there be for life in this world. Once again the question is not theoretical, abstract. It is a question of "going on." Why go on? With Goldie Hawn we ask, "What does it *all* mean?" Or again, the experience of our own temporality, the fact that our history and accomplishments lead so relentlessly to the grave—this experience asks with particular poignancy what the use of it all is. We will die. Someone else's energy and genius will take up where we left off, or even worse, will simply ignore what we have done and bury our life, our accomplishment, our history in that worst of all graveyards, forgetfulness. Perhaps not even a memory will remain. Once again, our sense of our own reality, our sense of our own meaning trembles on the brink. And once again, the nagging ultimate question, "Why go on?" Finally, within our own freedom, the fact that we reach out to others in love, that we set the most generous or heroic goals, that we set ethical standards for ourselves and our culture and work to make them a reality—all this only to find ourselves foundering on the sands of—*ourselves;* all of this, with the guilt, the alienation, the hostility and resentment toward the rest of the world, the "good guys," which flow out of our own moral impotence—all of this questions us radically, existentially. Why go on? Why try?

Transcendence

Two things should be pointed out here. The first is that these experiences—common, if not universal human experiences —constitute a *question*. The question is an existential, a practical question. Put in its simplest terms, it is "to be or not to be." But it *is* a question, which is to say that it is not an answer. On the contrary, it is the dissolution of an answer or a set of answers which we found sufficient justification to "keep us going." The point is that the question does not contain its own answer. Ultimate and radical questioning does not contain any one answer to the questioning. This may seem trite, but it is distressingly true that one is accused of "cheating in the language game" when one points out that religious use of language does refer to something within general human experience. Any number of answers are possible in the face of this questioning experience. One can simply refuse to admit the reality of a God other than the going cultural model. One can take the relative safety of the question and decide to adopt a Sartrian pose of heroic striving in the midst of absurdity. One can move to another relative framework and "deify" that. One can take the experience of others which leads to their "answer." Or one can take the difficult and dangerous trip for one's self. Why a person opts for any of these answers is a difficult question to answer, as difficult as the question why anyone really does anything. But we will come to one aspect of this later in this chapter.

The second thing to be pointed out is that this questioning constitutes an *invitation* to *transcendence*. It is an *invitation*. The spontaneous joy of suddenly finding one's self alive or the anxiety accompanying the collapse of any of the sets of meanings which gave solidity, significance and justification to one's self and one's world constitute what Gordon Kaufmann calls a "limit experience." What happens in these experiences is that for some reason we do pass beyond the limits of expectation or meaning we have set for ourselves—in an ecstasy of joy or anxiety—and become aware through this experience that our existence is framed by limits which we or someone or something else has set for us. Kaufmann uses the example of a man imprisoned in a cell. As long as he is truly imprisoned, he only knows the surface of the walls which close him in. Seeing that the depth of other things in his cell is limited, he might reason to the fact that the walls also could have a limit to their depth. But how deep are they? And what is on the other side? There is only one way to find out—to "climb up and over them" (*transcendere*). Of course, there are limits and limits and there is transcendence and transcendence. The questioning process to which we are referring, however, is a process of absolute, ultimate questioning. What does it *all* mean? What are we *all* about? In this process, every aspect of the empirical ego is relativized and everything, our accomplishments, our values, our significance, our very being, all of it is existentially questioned. "To be or not to be; that is the question."

As we have seen, there are any number of possible answers to this radical question. One can decide not to be. Finding everything which served as the framework for meaning and action to be so relative, so transitory can lead one to "his quietus make with a bare bodkin." One can take the Sartrian posture. One can idolize another framework. Or one can get to the bottom of the question. One can go beyond every aspect of the ego, and come to the place where one's life and every dimension of that life is found to be not of one's own construction, but radically "given." Teilhard's description of this kind of self-transcendence is already a classic.

> I took the lamp and, leaving the zone of everyday occupations and relationships where everything seems clear, I went down into my inmost self, to the deep abyss whence I feel dimly that my power emanates. But as I moved further and further away from the conventional certainties by which social life is superficially illuminated, I became aware that I was losing contact with myself. At each step of the descent, a new person was disclosed within me of whose name I was no longer sure and who no longer obeyed me. And when I had to stop my exploration because the path faded from beneath my steps, I found a bottomless abyss at my feet, and out of it— arising I knew not from where—the current which I dare call *my* life.
>
> . . . In the last resort the profound life, the fontal life, the newborn life, escape our grasp entirely.
>
> Stirred by my discovery, I then wanted to return to the light of day and forget the disturbing enigma in the comfortable surroundings of familiar things—to begin again living at the surface without imprudently plumbing the depths of the abyss. But then, beneath this very spectacle of the turmoil of life, there appeared, before my newly opened eyes, the

unknown that I wanted to escape. This time it was not hiding at the bottom of an abyss; it disguised its presence in the innumerable strands which form the web of chance, the very stuff of which the universe and my own small individuality are woven. Yet it was the same mystery without a doubt; I recognized it.[1]

This is only one description of the process by which the awareness of God becomes the transforming force in one's life. But it corresponds broadly with other descriptions of this difficult and dangerous (fraught with the possibilities of self-deception) process. And it is from this tradition that we receive whatever concrete experiential content can be given to the word "God." And this is the primary concern of this consideration: what, positively, does "God" mean?

The process which Teilhard and others describe is a process of *transcendence*. That is to say, it is a process in which we "climb up and over" the limits which our "ordinary" experience sets to our own reality and that of the world. The "facts" of everyday life are clear to us. They demand most or all of our attention and energy. Thus it is that we tend to consider them the "really real." Food on the table, money in the bank, clothes on our back, getting the job done—these are the things that occupy most of our waking (and even some of our dreaming) hours. Whatever is involved with, contributes to or detracts from these everyday realities is defined as the "relevant," what does not is consigned to the "irrelevant." The process of transcendence breaks out of these limits, passes beyond the identity we have as breadwinner, homemaker, rises above the roles we are assigned by the expectations family and society have of us to the awareness of who we really are in all these roles and functions. What is characteristic of the transcendence we are considering is its *totality*. It involves stripping away every mask of self-deception, going beyond any selfhood which can be de-

1. Teilhard de Chardin, P., *The Divine Milieu*, New York (Harper and Row: Harper Torchbook), 1968 (rev. ed.), p. 78.

fined in terms of accomplishments, failures or any other kind
of historical action (the *empirical ego*), going even beyond the
hidden but omnipresent unconscious or preconscious forces in
our lives. No longer do we experience ourselves as the one who
pretends to be good or bad, who has done this or that thing or
even the one subject to such or such a mysterious force in all
our action, good or bad.

This process of full or total self-transcendence consists then
in the progressive elimination of any identifiable or objectifiable
ground for our being. And, as such, it is a difficult, danger-
ously deceptive and often anguishing process. John of the
Cross's succession of *ni eso . . . ni eso . . . ni eso . . .* is not
simply a matter of theoretical or abstract options among which
one makes choices. Rather, it is a matter of successive and
deeper perceptions of the very reality of one's own personal
identity, realities which, in the last analysis, must all be rejected. It is a process of the progressive loss of "empirical ego,"
the very identifiability of one's self as a person. Further, it is a
simultaneous loss of "God" after "God," the god of the going
culture, the god who served as the explanation or justification
of any aspect of personal or corporate existence, the judging,
punishing god of the guilty, one by one, these and other gods
fall under John of the Cross's laconic statement *ni eso . . .
ni eso . . . ni eso.*

Perhaps the most suitable name for the experience of total
self-transcendence is "the experience of no-thing-ness." What
this means is that one transcends thing after thing as the center
of one's consciousness and identity. It becomes *experientially*
clear that one exists literally *ex nihilo*—out of no thing. No
particular or series of personal achievements, no person or
community, no conscious or unconscious goals or personal
farces—no *thing* is one's personal core. There is only, in Teilhard's words, an "abyss." It is, in Merton's words, "kenotic
transformation, an emptying of all the contents of the ego-
consciousness to become a void . . ." R. N. Bellah speaks of it
in terms of losing one's "home." Perhaps the best description
is in the pungent aphorism of Norman O. Brown, "I'm thou-

sands, I'm an in-divide-you-all, I'm no un (i.e., nun, no-un, no one)."[2] A long tradition refers to it as the final stage of "mortification," a "death to self."

It is extremely difficult to speak of this experience. Those who know most about it, mystical or Zen masters, resort to poetry, aphorism, paradox—anything to break down the human propensity for objectification and security. Norman O. Brown simply says, "The solution to the problem of identity is, get lost. Or as it says in the New Testament: He that findeth his own psyche shall lose it, and he that loseth his psyche for my sake shall find it."[3] However, it does seem that there are some aspects of the experience which can be described and that these have significant implications for the understanding of what sacramental religion is all about in the last analysis.

First, there is the paradoxical fact that it is in the process of self-transcendence, in the loss of control, the loss of the empirical ego that the truest "self" is found. One no longer sees one's self as constituted by achievement, opinions, relations. True, all of these do constitute the empirical identity of the person who accepts this experience. But in transcending these one discovers one's self as not tied to one's past, full of almost infinite possibilities. One comes to accept the deep mystery of one's "own" life and in accepting this mystery, one breaks the bonds which past and present place around the possibilities of the future. The relativization of every objective value serves, in the most paradoxical way, to integrate one at one's "deepest" level in a liberating transformation. Our history is still our own. We can confess with "religious" depth and conviction, "*I have* achieved this or that. *I have* done this or that cruel, ugly, sinful thing." But none of these exhausts the deep mystery and rich possibility we really are. And in this way we can come to love ourselves in the full acceptance of who we are, what we have done and what we can be, love

2. *Love's Body*. New York (Random House: Vintage Books) 1966, p. 160.

3. *Op. cit.*, p. 161.

ourselves not only for the good things we have done or achieved, but love ourselves even in the recognition and acceptance of the evil we have done.

Second, the fruit of self-transcendence is a quality of vision and, therefore, of experience. And, in this sense, self-transcendence effects a new consciousness. Thus, if we define "person" in terms of subjectivity, we can say that this new quality of vision, experience and consciousness brings about a "new person." One does not see more "things" but rather sees everything there is to see in a different way, against a different horizon. Of course, this implies a difference in action, but it is important to stress that this ethical implication is rooted in a change of vision. There is a "new heart," a "new spirit" which is the center for vision, experience, choice and action.

Third, it is out of this quality of vision and experience that the reality of God emerges. What emerges is *not an object*. One does not develop a kind of X-ray vision in which a hidden object is grasped or perceived. What emerges in experience is rather a structure, a dynamism, a horizon out of which and in terms of which everything else is seen. And the same background out of which one perceives everything is seen to be the dynamism which permeates all objective reality. Teilhard describes well how the reality which is the all-permeating horizon of one's personal being is seen as the horizon against which everything else is seen and which is the all-permeating reality of everything else. But one thing is clear and of capital importance—no-thing emerges. God is not an object, a thing. Rather God is the dynamism in terms of which (whom?) everything is what it is in every aspect of its being. We might use the example of one's own personal reality. It is not a thing. It is, in Teilhard's words, an "abyss" out of which every aspect of personal being emerges. But because it is the type of reality it is, it is all-permeating of every aspect of our being. In other words, our personal reality *transcends* every individual aspect and dimension of our personal history, but *precisely because* it is the transcendent reality, it is deeply *immanent* in every other aspect of our personal life.

We might put this in other words. When we open ourselves to the experience of nothingness in total self-transcendence, we don't get The Answer. Hopefully, The Answer gets us.

Put in more biblical language, out of the "Spirit of God," the "Word of God" emerges as the *Logos* of all reality. Teilhard puts this well when he speaks of the "radiance" of the divine milieu which changes nothing in the relationships between things, but bathes the world with an inward light "which intensifies its relief, its structure and its depth.... If we may slightly alter a hallowed expression, we could say that the great mystery of Christianity is not exactly the appearance, but the transparence of God in the universe. *Yes, Lord, not only the ray that strikes the surface, but the ray that penetrates, not only your Epiphany, Jesus, but your diaphany.*"[4] We neither "put God there" nor do we "perceive God there" as a hidden object; rather, we reach the vantage point from which, to cite Teilhard again, "not only his vision but things themselves radiate . . . the subjective viewpoint coincides with the way things are distributed objectively, and perception reaches its apogee. The landscape lights up and yields its secrets. He sees."[5]

Once again, what is seen is not a thing. To cite from Teilhard's prayer,

> Truly . . . in the continually beneficent play of secondary causes, I touch, as near as possible, the two faces of your creative action, and I encounter and kiss, your two marvelous hands—the one which holds us so firmly that it is merged, in us, with the sources of life, and the other whose embrace is so wide that, at its slightest pressure, all the springs of the universe respond harmoniously together.[6]

4. *The Divine Milieu,* pp. 130–131.
5. Teilhard de Chardin, P., *The Phenomenon of Man,* New York (Harper and Row: Harper Torchbook), 1956², p. 32.
6. *The Divine Milieu,* pp. 78–79.

What is seen is one's self and everything else—but differently. The horizon against which it is seen is a reality which is, in Augustine's words, *intimior intimo meo* (more interior than my own deepest interior). Like our own very subjectivity, it is not seen, but forms the background against which everything else is seen, against which every aspect of ourselves sees and acts. It is a transcendent reality seen precisely because of its transcendence in every aspect of what is real. What is important about this conclusion is that the Transcendent emergent from self-transcendence *changes nothing*. Cold is cold, hot is hot, pain is still pain and joy is still joy. And yet *everything* is changed in that the vision we come to possess gives to things we see and encounter their truest depth and solidity. The distinction between subject and object is overcome. We are one with ourselves, one with our world and in a transforming and liberating background of vision and action. And in this sense we can become truly "religious" in the sense in which E. Schillebeeckx describes religion, "letting God *be God* in our lives."[7]

Problems

Of course, there are difficulties with everything that has been said up to this point. A priest could well ask how he would stand in a pulpit and tell his congregation that ultimately their assembling there was about nothing. A teacher would well ask how he or she could point out to their class that religion is ultimately about nothing. A believer could well ask whether sacramental religion is finally about nothing. (In fact, growing numbers of people seem to think this, but in another sense.) But that would be a misinterpretation of what has been said. We are dealing with God—the ultimate reality, the ultimate "object" of religion, and simply pointing out that God is not an object to be grasped,

7. "De zin van het mean-zijn van Jesus, de Christus" in *Tijdschrift voor Theologie* 2 (1962), p. 129.

delivered or "handled" in any way. We are dealing with what classical theology called the "incomprehensibility" of God, the fact that God is not "grasped" like any other object of knowledge and that any human knowledge of God is only mediate and indirect. Classical theology spoke of the "light" by which God is known more directly, but did not detail the concrete experience in which this "light" dawns. Those who specialized in the more experiential and concrete ways of meeting the reality of God spoke of "darkness" rather than "light," of the "cloud," the cloud of "un-knowing," the cloud that lights up the dark.

The pragmatic value of this tradition might well be questioned. After all there is a kind of "nihilism" which has led to the tragic posturings of a Nietzsche or a Sartre, and which forms the basis for so much of what is most violent and destructive in today's revolutionary movements. But this kind of nihilism is a reaction to the collapse of so many values which were once accepted as "God-given" and whose demise leaves no visible option except that of the fruitless emptiness of negation, destruction or violence, a kind of *Götterdämmerung* for culture and its values, a fire which consumes all and leaves nothing.

However, this kind of nihilism is only a caricature of the authentic nihilism which is the fruit of self-transcendence. Our existence and that of all of our world is founded on what we can only experience as an abyss, a reality so totally "other" from us that we can only give it experiential content by calling it no-thing. Far from being a threat or bondage for our freedom, the emergence of this reality from our own experience of nothingness is the only source and stimulus for real freedom. To live in real freedom, we must return to that place and experience again and again. For it is only there that we can see, know and love ourselves and our world in a way that is free of the limits of our and its past, open to the practically infinite possibilities of our and its future. Only out of that place and experience can we really dare all. For it is only in letting go of every-thing and giving ourselves to the All that we can *experience* the fact that God is the One who gives us our lives as *our very own,* our action as our very own. And there we really know that God will not step in to patch up after our mistakes, that we are really free, really responsible.

Another pragmatic problem has to do with the certainty of the outcome of the process of transcendence. Will the reality of God emerge from every process of self-transcendence? Is there any guarantee that the loss of personal or corporate empirical ego will face us with The Answer? The answer to these questions is obvious to anyone who has surveyed even cursorily the history of human thought and action. The options of theism, antitheism and atheism are always there. Skepticism and various forms of nihilism are just as common as liberated renewals of faith in those periods where the structures of personal and corporate self-justification pass through their periods of decline and death. The accepted theism of an earlier age or period of history either matures with the integration of new experience or it dies in the out-of-hand rejection of the past which opts for skepticism of nihilism. And why theism matures or deteriorates is difficult to say with any certainty at all. However, one thing does seem clear and important at this point. And this is that, given the structures of human knowledge, judgment and action, we cannot expect anyone to respond with mature affirmation to the goodness and meaningfulness of existence if that person's whole experience of life and other people is negative. True, we might believe in miracles, but we should never count on them. If the whole horizon for knowledge, interpretation and judgment is overcast with negativity, one cannot reasonably expect mature affirmative commitment. What this means concretely for sacramental religion is that it cannot expect to make up by ritual what is lacking on a broad scale in a person's life. Sacramental religion ministers to a far broader framework, the framework of human existence itself, and seeks in its ministry to facilitate the possibility of "belief in God." The sacramental community is called upon to be a horizon of affirmation and hope for its members so that the inevitable "shocks" which raise the question of being or not being can be faced by each of its members as experiences laden with possibility for a growing openness to the reality of God rather than experiences which are simply negative and destructive. Everyone who lives without hope or faith in the sacramental community, everyone who leaves that community because hope and faith have died is a "judgment" on the truth and spirit of the community itself. "Let a man examine himself and so eat of the bread and drink of the cup." (1 Cor 11:28)

A final practical problem has to do with the reasonableness of what has been said up to this point. How available is the experience of nothingness and self-transcendence? How much "nothing" can people take? The real answer to this is that the experience is as available as we are willing and able to make it and we can stand as much nothing as we are willing and able to stand. We must be either very dense indeed or so myopically oriented toward security that we are almost blind if we cannot see the relativity and temporality of our achievements. We live in a time which is peculiarly aware of these, when social, political and religious institutions experience such tension between the safety of the traditional and the crying need for renewal. The problem, personally and corporately, is whether we can accept, even welcome this invitation to transcendence which lies in the cultural and personal shocks which call attention to our personal and corporate relativity and temporality. Our achievements and ourselves *will* pass away, *are* passing away. That is a fact. Whether we can accept and welcome this fact as more real than the relative and temporal achievements of our lives depends on whether we see this relativity as a threat to everything or as an invitation to go deeper, beyond achievement, beyond ego to the abyss on which our lives rest. The willingness to accept and welcome it is the first condition for the availability of the experience.

Speaking more ontologically, but out of the experience of relativity and temporality, we can define specifically human existence as spirit, as an on-going process of inquiry. The very reflective character of our existence, our natural drive to see our activity as our own, to reflect on it, evaluate it—all this means that every aspect of our personal history is open to question, to transcendence—every aspect, that is, except the questioning itself. That is simply there. Thus, the experience of nothingness and the invitation to self-transcendence which it contains are not only available, they are the very fabric of our being human.

But this already has something important to say to our sacramental religion. For if sacramental religion is a celebration of *who we are* in Christ, we celebrate this nothingness on which our lives are founded and the transcendence of God which is revealed there. The function of sacramental religion, an attitude toward God celebrated in cultic profession, is precisely to facilitate the acceptance of this invitation. Our function is to minister to the quality of consciousness which emerges from this acceptance, the consciousness which makes the "diaphany" of God possible. If God is the central reality in Jesus, His Christ, in the Church which is gathered together in His Spirit, it seems quite clear that sacramental ministry and sacramental religion are basically concerned with this vision, this transcendence. The principal function of religion and its sacramental expression is to issue the invitation to each believer to open himself or herself to the basic question we all are. Far from settling us in security, religion should be the principal stimulus to a continual transcendence of any or all of the achievements which define a personal or corporate ego.

But the practical problem still remains. How much "nothing" can people take? This is a question of the ability one has to accept and welcome the experience of nothingness in one's life and culture as a liberating experience, to enter into the process of self-transcendence in freedom, in responsible creativity. And of course, this will vary from person to person for as many individual reasons as there are persons. Basically, this is a mystery. It is an actuality over which only the free person himself has any control at all. Only the free person himself can progressively determine how far he can go beyond any given boundaries and limits of achievement and security, to what extent he is willing to question every past achievement, every present reality and go beyond to a new reality in responsible creativity. It is up to the free person to determine to what extent the reality of God, the background of any experience of nothingness, will emerge in his life. It is up to the free person to determine how deeply that background will permeate his vision and action. In a meditation entitled *Perdre la foi* (To Lose the Faith) G. Lemercier puts the following words in the mouth of Jesus:

> Gregoire, one day I said, "Whoever seeks to save his life will lose it, and whoever loses it will find it." I could just as well have said, "whoever seeks to save his faith will lose it and whoever loses it will find it," because faith is like the soul of life.
>
> Gregoire, you should lose your faith, continually, if you want to save it. Not that it is possible simply to "lose the faith," no, but you should lose the limits which your belief, which is the support of your faith, bring to your faith to the point where belief imprisons faith. This is a task to take up day after day, a task which will make you pass constantly between the feelings of fear and liberation.
>
> Myself, I passed through that great adventure. Otherwise, I would not have been a man, your brother. Remember my cry on the cross, when I confronted my mountain, death, "My God, My God, why have you forsaken me?"
>
> And do not forget, Gregoire, the disciple is no greater than his master.[8]

How far one can actually go in this process not only depends on the individual but also depends on the mysterious things which take place in the process. In Zen, there is a point, satori.

8. Le Mercier, G., *Dialogues avec le Christ*. Paris (Editions Bernard Grasset) 1966, p. 231.

There, one can say, "This is it." This is not true in the Christian
interpretation of self-transcendence. The place of nothingness
must be visited over and over again to transform and relativize
even our most "spiritual" achievements. Even these can be
turned into idols which inhabit the sanctuary of the depths of
our being. There is one term however—death. That is the ultimate decision to open one's self to complete transcendence,
leaving every gain or achievement behind, in the ultimate
creative transformation of the whole of life. But how far the
reality of God can penetrate human freedom (i.e., how deeply
a person can be graced) is basically a matter of how far a person
will let that reality penetrate. Not everyone has the ability or
the time to allow themselves to be so completely dominated by
that presence that there is nothing else in life. But the fact still
remains that real freedom, responsibility and creativity involve
some occurrence of the experience of nothingness. Without it
we are locked into an "eternal" set of values, practices, convictions. Our lives simply cease to be our own.

Once again, all this has something very fundamental to say
about sacramental religion. If sacramental religion has to do
ultimately with man's relation to God, then it must face this
fundamental fact: That the place where man comes closest to
God is in the experiences of nothingness, in the transcending
of the limits which form the "home" for any particular stage
of our lives. And accordingly, sacramental religion is ultimately
at the service of man in terms of this process of self-transcendence. "The sabbath was made for man, not man for the sabbath." (Mk 2:27) Concretely, this means that ritual, preaching
should aim primarily at the facilitation of the acceptance and
welcoming of the experiences of nothingness in which man questions himself deeply and grows through this questioning toward
the "new heart" and "new spirit" in which he comes closer to
the reality of the "living God." This also means that the ultimate
test of the "efficacy" of sacramental practice is, "Does it work?"
Does sacramental religion really serve man in his relation to
God? Does it help man to go beyond the values, securities and

achievements of any particular stage of his development? Or is it, in the last analysis, only at its own service?

Conclusions

The conclusions to what has been said are probably obvious but it is helpful to state them explicitly in order to have before us as clearly as possible what sacramental religion is in the last analysis.

First, in moving from the experiential content of our speaking of "God" to a concept of "God," rather than *vice versa,* a significant change takes place. Rather than an *object* of our experience, we find that our speaking of God signifies a special kind of experience. This has been characterized as the experience of "nothingness" both because there is no thing, no categorical object for the experience as well as because the human experience out of which the awareness of the reality of God arises is the experience of "nothingness," that departure from the stable, the given, the secure which takes place in the questioning of one's own being. Our awareness of God, in other words, is situated in the kind of human experience which the awareness of our own contingency, relativity or temporality creates within us. The reason for adopting this movement in thinking about God is the contemporary question which is no longer "Is there a God or is there not?" but "What does 'God' mean?" Here we are faced with the problem of showing that our language does signify some experiential fact which it brings to expression and communicates. Thus, when we speak of "God," we are speaking of an unfathomable depth revealed to us through a depth in our own lives which transcends any of our own action and achievement. We are speaking of that "groundless ground" which forms the horizon of every aspect of our understanding and action. We are speaking of that reality which informs every aspect of ourselves and our world, but which eludes capturing within any or all of these. In this sense, we are speaking of the most mysterious content of ourselves and our world.

Second, it is apparent from this significance of our speaking about God that our sacramental religion does not "deliver God" to the believer. This does not mean that sacraments are fruitless or powerless. What it does mean is that there is no object-God in the possession of the ritual or minister of the sacraments. What fruit and power the sacraments do possess lies in their power to renew in the community and the individual within the community that place where they are related to the reality of God, the experience of nothingness and the invitation to transcendence and through transcendence to the Transcendent which that experience contains.

Third, it is apparent, then, that the power of sacraments and consequently the purpose of their existence is to be understood in terms of a *quality of consciousness* whose facilitation and development is their fundamental function. The consciousness in question is not simply a speculative awareness for purposes of interpretation (although it is this latter also) but a practical consciousness which includes the capacity to see, experience and act. This quality of consciousness which is the fruit of self-transcendence does not remove one from the everyday world, but reveals in that world deeper and deeper dimensions of meaning. There is, in other words, a deepening of one's faith in one's self, the world and the God who permeates all in transcendent immanence. No *thing* is physically changed by this vision. Hot is hot, cold is cold, poor is poor, rich is rich, good is good and bad is bad. But in all of these the reality and designs of God appear. Thus, the reality of the everyday world is experienced differently, and one responds to it differently. The basic concern of the vision of this faith is for the freedom, love and dignity to which the transcendently immanent God calls all. Of course, this consciousness, vision and the consequent experience are neither automatic nor easy. This quality of consciousness demands greater and greater fidelity to the questioning, deep questioning process that defines our very humanness. And, as wonderful as it may sound in the abstract, this is something we simply find difficult to do. Yet it is precisely in this process and in its fruits in our lives that, although we cannot deliver God, God, hopefully and with infinite respect for our freedom and un-freedom, will "deliver" Himself to us.

Fourth, with this absolutely fundamental consideration, any inclination to vest "magic" powers in sacramental religion is precluded at the very outset. This, once again, does not mean that sacraments are without efficacy, without power. The divine sanction for their power is given to us in the words in which Jesus associates Himself with the name God gave to Moses. On Horeb, when Moses asked God for His name, God answered, "I will be there with you; with all that I am I will be there." (Ex 3:14) On the "mountain to which Jesus had directed them," Jesus said, "I am with you always, to the close of the age." (Mt 28:20) But this being-there must always be seen in the light of the fact that we are free to accept, ignore or actively reject this transcendent presence. Further, this presence is transcendent, i.e., it is an all-pervading presence, immanent in every aspect of reality which can only be perceived if we have the consciousness and vision to perceive it. In other words, it does not have a separate categorical function and power but comes to meet us enfleshed in the depths of other persons and our world. All we can do with respect to this presence and power ordinarily (a discussion of miracles would take us too far afield) is let it be-there.

What all this means is that the power of sacraments, granted it is divine power, operates within the dynamics of the symbolic function of the believing community. We cannot, therefore, put blind faith in traditional ritual with the confidence that "God will take care of it." Rather than relying on the legalistic tradition of the "validity" of sacraments, we would do far better to return to the older tradition of the "truth" of the sacramental sign. For this approach is not simply concerned with legal acceptability of sacraments, but goes further to take into consideration how sacraments really function in the relationship of the believer with God (grace). In this context, the power of sacramental action corresponds to the truth of the sign-act. And the truth in question lies first of all in the fidelity of the community profession of faith to the actual human situation. Thus, sacraments have power to truly relate man to God if the faith-profession in terms of Community, spirit, celebration, forgiveness, concern and support actually reflects the *de facto* structure and processes of human existence and development. The question of truth here is, "Is what we profess in this common profession of faith faithful to the reality we all are, or is it not?" In this light, there is a demand for an on-going reflection on the actualities of the human situation and an accommodation of sacramental religion to those actualities. The understanding of human existence of one century does not necessarily reflect the later, hopefully more developed, appreciation of what it means to be man. And, secondly, within this framework the question of the fidelity of external expression to internal attitude: "Does this profession of faith actually bring to expression a real fidelity to the faith of the community, or is it merely an empty ritual action?" A faith can only be deepened in its being brought to expression if the faith is really there. But even given both of these "truths" in sacramental worship, we still remain free. The community can only stand on the threshold of our freedom; the community can only invite, it cannot force our freedom.

From this it is apparent that sacramental action is essentially *hopeful* action. It is a common sharing of faith *in the hope of* the acceptance and deepening of faith in decision and commitment. We will consider this more fully in our reflection on the theme of community, but we can point out here that it is a question of *realistic* hope. There is an attitude, "optimism," which goes by the name of hope but which, in reality, can be nothing more than wishful thinking wrapped up in delusion. The hope in question here is neither optimistic nor pessimistic. These are "faiths," general views of the world and human existence which prejudge and limit possibilities. Hope in the "living God" can only be based on truth, honesty and realism. And this realism must take into account both the freedom and lack of freedom of the members of the community of faith and those to whom and for whom the community brings its faith to cultic expression.

Fifth and finally, since the theme of God is the most fundamental and governing consideration in sacramental religion and theology, it would seem that the significance of God in the life of the believer should be the governing principle for the propriety of the symbolic (liturgical) forms in which the community of belief expresses its faith. This would imply that a Church should be ready to continually transcend any given cultural expression of its faith in liturgical forms. We know that this is not the case at present. Karl Mannheim. commenting on the history of the Prussian regimes, has some illuminating remarks on "bureaucratic thinking." Pointing out that the bureaucrat's sphere of action lies within the limits of already formulated laws, Mannheim explains that the fundamental tendency of bureaucratic thought is to treat all problems as problems of administration, problems which are solved by decree, rescript and memo. Any swelling of new forces in a society is handled by arbitrary decree in terms of an order of law which the bureaucrat considers to be the only and total order possible. To expect the functionary to be a creative force in the process of development and change is simply to expect too much. This sounds very familiar when we view the problems of renewal after Vatican II. C. J. McNaspy points to the problem when he writes that what is needed at this time are not changes, but change. The question for sacramental and liturgical theology is, "Can we transcend our own liturgical forms, or have we so idolized them that we invest them with the immutability of God Himself?" If the reality of God in the life of the believer is the fundamental principle of sacramental theory and liturgical practice, the norm for the suitability of any given practice becomes more pragmatic. Does this really and effectively invite and facilitate the quality of consciousness in which the reality of God is approached in personal corporate self-transcendence, or does it not?

Spirit

What has been seen in our reflection on the meaning of "God" in terms of human experience can be resumed and deepened by placing it in the context of what we mean by "spirit." The reason for this is that the process of self-transcendence and the event of our being taken over by a new and more revealing horizon for vision, understanding and action are precisely what we mean when we speak of ourselves or of God as "spirit." In our reflection on this theme, we want to deepen some of the preceding reflections on God in terms of our openness to and union with God and God's union with us in terms of our understanding of ourselves as spirit, of God as Spirit and Spirit as God. This will serve as a prelude for our reflection on the meaning of Jesus, the Christ. Of course, the context of all this is specifically *sacramental,* i.e., concerned with the experiential content of our sacramental religious practice. We are concerned here, ultimately, with sacramental *meaning,* which is nothing more nor less than the interior content of our symbolic religious action. Thus, our question for this theme is: "How do we experience ourselves as spirit and God as Spirit?"

It might be well to start negatively, with what "spirit" does not mean, at least in these reflections. For many of us, perhaps, the mention of "spirit" summons up the eerie connotation of "spook" or "ghost." Spirit is a spirit out of the past, the shade or memory of one who was once embodied like ourselves but who no longer exists in bodily form. The past history of the spirit gives it a shape, so we picture it, devoid of our own fleshy condition, but still somehow identifiable. It has an objectifiable shape, something there to be seen, like a television "ghost." Like an airy counterpart of its earlier historical shape, it hovers there, comes and goes mysteriously, frightens us by its strangeness. Certainly this image of spirit is useful for our imagining of that imperishable part of ourselves and our history which lives on after the material aspect of our personal being returns to the cycles of earthly composition and decomposition. But this image of spirit is unsatisfactory precisely because of its frozenness in the past and its objective shape. Our concern here is for an understanding of what it means for any of us (and for God) to be spirit *now*. And for this it is not enough to rest content with the ghost of our former selves (or God's former self).

"Spirit" also brings to mind the "spiritual." It means the better self we would all like to be but are not because of our "fleshy" selves. We are most spirit, most spiritual when we are doing what is right or holy, overcoming our flesh, praying, going to church. There is nothing wrong with thinking of spirit and the spiritual in this way. St. Paul speaks this way when he distinguishes those who live by the "flesh" and its work and those who live by the spirit and its work (Rom 8:12; Gal 5:16 ff.). This is a valid and meaningful division of Christians (and every Christian) into good guys and bad guys. But we want to reflect on the meaning of spirit in broader human terms. What does it mean for anyone at any time to be spirit? And what does it mean for God to be Spirit?

The problem with both the reality of "ghost" and that of "spiritual" is that they are all too easily objectified. They are too easily seen as something which is "already out there," over against us with an objective content. However, as will emerge from our reflection, spirit is the most nonobjective reality of all. Spirit never reveals itself but is, rather, that in which and through which everything else is revealed, everything else is seen. We could use a few other expressions to clarify what we mean by spirit. Spirit is *horizon*. A horizon is not a thing which lies within the scope of our vision. It is there, it is true, but it is not an object which we see. Rather it is the limit of vision which situates everything else which we can see. It is a fluid reality—the broader our horizon, the more we can see and the more different the perspective from which we can see and appreciate what we see. From one place we have one horizon and from a "higher" place, we have a different horizon, see more and appreciate its location differently. So we can move from one place to another and as we move things are seen and appreciated differently. Thus, depending on the breadth and quality of spirit (a greater or lesser capacity to see) we can see more or less, see with greater or less breadth. Again, a good word for spirit would be *background*. A background, like a horizon, is that against which everything is seen and appreciated. But this word, especially if we understand it as a personal and subjective reality, brings out the fact that the same thing can be seen differently against different backgrounds. Spirit doesn't see more or less things; it sees the same things differently depending on the quality of vision which is developed. It lies ever on this side of what is seen, a deeply subjective and personal principle. Teilhard uses a good expression for spirit: *milieu*. Milieu means two things in French. First, it is the center, the middle of something. In this sense, spirit is our center, the deepest dimension of our existence, out of which we see and experience the world around us and out of which we act. But milieu also means a setting in which things are situated, in which action takes place, like a set on a stage. It is a context, a background which gives a particular focus to what is seen taking place. And these two meanings are not unrelated. The only reason why a scene is "set" is the center of vision and evaluation of the artist who creates the drama. The real "set" is in the vision and interpretation of the playwright. Likewise, as Teilhard remarks in his description of "seeing," the "seer" finds himself at the center of everything he sees. It is from his milieu that things are seen *in the way they are seen.*

Context for Living

Thus, spirit is a reality, but it is not an object of vision or experience. Rather, it is the personal, historical background, horizon, perspective against which everything else is seen in a particular way. Spirit gives the tone and meaning to what is seen. Take the Russians. To a professional anti-Communist, they are a plague in the world, an evil, dominating, oppressive force which seeks to enslave the world in the name of a godless ideology. To a sympathetic pro-Communist viewer, they are a progressive, liberating force seeking to free man from the patterns of economic oppression. The same object, but a different reality of vision, experience and action. Thus, the experience of spirit is a deeply personal experience which gives a particular and personal quality to our vision, our experience and our action in the world. We will reflect on the experience, then, in terms of five aspects of this experience: the experience of consciousness, the experience of inner time, the experience of freedom, the experience of hope and what Von Hildebrand calls the "we-experience."

Consciousness. Our experience of consciousness gives us a certain discontinuity with the rest of the world around us. We own ourselves and own the world around us in a very special way. We look out on the world and in on ourselves and we feel a peculiar mastery of it all simply because we can say, "I am, you are, he, she or it is." There are the stones and there is the running brook. The problem for them is that they don't know that they are there. We do. So we can hear the sermon from the stones and read the book in the running brook, but they can neither hear nor read each other. The stone can only stand solidly against the pressure of the flowing water and the brook can only bend its fluidity around the surface of the stone. No sermons, no books there. What puts the books and sermons there is our capacity to be conscious of our own consciousness. Only the human being can be conscious of being and say, "I am." No other brand of being can make that claim. And that simple expression shows the transcendent difference between the human and the rest of the world. It shows us that our very existence reveals itself to us and makes its claim on us. Brooks and stones can be present one to another in a certain physical, spatial contiguity, but we have a self-presence which reveals a profoundly greater depth to our personal reality. Our presence to ourselves, our capacity to make our own existence the object of our thinking, planning, hope or despair gives us the power to penetrate ever deeper into the incredible richness of our own human life, to become more and more intensely present to ourselves. And because we can be conscious of and relate to ourselves in this way, we can relate to the whole world on a deeper and more significant level than that of mere physical interaction. Because of our conscious experience of our own existence, our past, our present, our future, we can direct our concern, our wonder, our hope or fear to the existence of everything around us. Because we can say, "I am," we can also say, "That is," and this is no mere statement of neutral fact. It is a statement full of revelation, claim and challenge.

As spirit, then, we are constantly confronted with ourselves and a world which becomes "our" world because of the way in which we can relate to it and to ourselves. And this confrontation is a confrontation, not simply a matter of ourselves or our world simply being there, to be observed in some bland neutrality. We must constantly do something about ourselves, about our world. Thus it is that "to be or not to be" is not simply a question we have, it is a question we are. It is a question out of which, whether we like it or not, we must question everything. This means that as spirit, by the continuous confrontation with ourselves and our world which the experience of consciousness brings to us, we are very restless beings indeed. As we seek out meaning, value, truth, it is really our own meaning, our own value, our own truth which is our quest and question in the search for and creation of the process we call our "being," our "life." Thus, spirit is a question, an open question, and our deepest truth lies not so much in the discovery of any one answer which closes off our questing and questioning and thus lets us off the hook, but rather in the faithfulness with which we seek after our own life and being as it constantly calls to us from our future. To be spirit, then, i.e., to really *be* spirit, is all a matter of openness, openness to our selves, to the question and question we are, constantly in search of ourselves and our world. To be human is to be on a quest, to be questing, questioning. Of course, appearances can be deceiving. Not everything that looks human really is human all the time. We can and do refuse our own humanity, the humanity of others when we refuse to really *be* our own questing and question, when we refuse to let others be their questing and question. Spirit in search of itself is a constant quest for more being, but we all know how easy it is to settle for the comfort of well-being, to settle into a fixed and secure framework for our existence, to let a force within us which demands movement become confined, closed in, dead air rather than a free-moving wind. In N. O. Brown's way of seeing it, we prefer the holy ghost to the *creator spiritus*.

Time. This experience of consciousness brings us to the second important aspect of our existence as spirit, the sense of time. It is important to begin with what we do not mean by time. Science has a way of looking at time as a measurement—the measurement of the rate of succession of various physical phenomena. This is a clinical, neutral attitude which observes changes taking place and measures the rate by which one state succeeds another. This is an "out there" kind of time. It was there as long as matter existed and will be there as long as matter continues to exist and to undergo any kind of change. As Myrt used to say to Marge, "Stuff happens" and "stuff" will continue to happen, maybe forever. So time was always there and maybe there will always be time. The Greeks have a word for this—*chronos;* and the chronology of material events stretches back into the past and indefinitely into the future— there will always be time. We know where the physical history of the world has brought us and we can more or less predict where it will go. So time is out there and the future is already made, as by some known or unknown series of causes the history of the physical universe will go on. And all that matters about us is that somehow we are part of this on-going process. We come and go—we hope for a better, timeless existence—but the world goes on. So time is a shackle, locking us into a relentless pattern of change in which we have little or no significance. No spirit, no humanity there. So we look for salvation from this kind of slavery in a "timeless," eternal kind of existence which frees us from this heartless juggernaut. But this is precisely what we do not mean by our experience of time.

Spirit's experience of time is an experience of time over which we are to have mastery, a time which we make rather than a time which simply masters us. Our experience of time, to the extent that it is the time of spirit, and not just a brutish kind of time, is based on the necessity of "doing something" about ourselves, about our world. We must do something about ourselves now. But who are we now? We are precisely the ones we have made ourselves to be. Our decisions (and our refusals to decide) from the past live on in who we are right now, giving us a definite concrete capacity to make the decisions now which will make us be who we will be tomorrow and into the future. We can't do everything, we can only do what we can do, and what we can do is rooted in what we have done. But all that we have done and have become is a matter which we must face over and over again, is something we must do something about. Thus, spirit's experience of time is not simply an experience of *the* past, *the* present or *the* future; it is an experience of *our* past, *our* present, *our* future. Our experience of our time is an experience of a constant dialogue with ourselves, with our very existence. What's to be done, where shall we go? The Greeks have a word for this too—*kairos:* a moment in time when a decision must be made (The hour has come!). Thus, rather than being a mere *chrono*logy, our time is a *kairo*logy, an experience of a time which is ours, made ours by the people we become and want to become by doing something about ourselves and our world, a time made of and for decision, a time which is not the neutral object of observation, but the very personal content of who we have become and who we will be. *Our* time is an experience of our existence, our own life making its claim on us, facing us with the concrete possibilities of action because of who we have become and demanding that we move into *our* future by our own decision and action.

Freedom. Thus, spirit is being a constant call to action, decision, a summons to more being. However, what we do in fact in any decision or action depends on another dimension of the experience of being spirit—the experience of freedom. What is important to keep in mind here is that we are speaking of the *experience* of freedom. It's true that we can syllogize very easily; all men are free and I am a man, therefore I am free, but this is a far cry from the experience of freedom. It is at best an abstract intellectual tenet which can be empty indeed. We can hold to this conviction with utter logical clarity and still experience ourselves as hopelessly locked into a pattern of inner un-freedom (fears, compulsions, tensions) and relentless coercion by the forces of nature, culture, politics, family, religion and so on. Rather than experiencing ourselves as spirit, owning and facing the demands of our existence, we are quite thoroughly owned by forces which make it difficult if at all possible to truly say "I am." To be, in this case, is to be run, run by merciless masters, fear, desire, conformity. This, while we mutter our abstract logic: All men are free, I am a man, therefore I am free.

The experience of freedom is, in fact, an experience of liberation. It happens when either because of our own personal struggles or because of some surprising "miracle" some of the bonds we have just mentioned are broken and we find ourselves able to move into a new area of existence unfettered by those things which formerly limited our vision, our experience or our action. Suddenly or finally, we can say "I am" in a new and larger way. Somehow we have climbed up and over (transcended) some of the things in ourselves or around us which have locked our vision, our experience, our action into the predictable patterns of habit, conformity or any inner or outer force which makes us one with the "stuff" that always has and always will happen. Like it or not (and we do sometimes prefer our chains! —*cella continuata dulcescit:* if you live long enough in your cell it gets to be a nice place), new possibilities and new actualities are revealed; things, we ourselves can be different, better, larger. The experience of freedom is the actual experience of the "more being" for which spirit is a constant cry. To be freed is to be more, more spirit, more human.

It is true that we can gain this freedom, this enlargement of our existence, by our own inner struggles with all that seeks within us to diminish our existence in freedom. Through whatever kind of discipline, we can work to gain Meister Eckhart's "clear eye" in order to be able to see the full truth of our own selves, a truth which makes us free if we follow it faithfully. But it is probably more true to say that the greatest and most common freeing force in human life is the force of love. As Snoopy says, "A friend is someone who takes the leash off!" And Paul tells us, "You have not received the spirit of slavery to fall back into fear . . . the Spirit bears witness to our spirit that we are children (*liberi!*) of God" (Rom 8:15–16). But the fruit by which we gain the spirit which makes us God's freeborn children is known by its fruits within our experience, "the fruit of the spirit is love, joy, peace, patience, kindness, goodness, faithfulness, gentleness, self-control . . ." (Gal 5:22).

The path of the solitary ascetic has a long and distinguished history, some of it bad, but some of it also very good. But it is generally recognized that it is not a way for everyone, and probably only for relatively few people. It is fraught with the dangers of illusion and self-deception. Indeed, one great master of the life of spirit, Ignatius of Loyola, thought that most people (nine out of ten!) who give themselves to long prayers are fooling themselves. And the long chapters on the different ways in which we are deceived in the life of the spirit which form a good part of any treatment of the life of the spirit worth its salt should warn us of the difficulty and dangers of the lonely way. Thus it would seem fairly obvious that for most of us, it is the way of love which leads most commonly to the liberation which makes us more and more spirit, less and less "flesh." For it is of the power of love more than any other human (or divine) force to really free us, open us up to more being and, in this sense, make us more spirit. For it is the power of love more than any other which can evoke our spirit, call us forth from the cozy cells (or tombs) in which we wall up our existence to keep us safe from the frightening demands of our very humanity.

The experience of freedom, then, is not the conviction of an abstract human quality, not even of a God-given human right. To the extent that freedom is a reality in human experience, it is an experience of passing beyond the real or imagined obstacles to being truly human, truly ourselves, truly spirit. It is a real liberation from limits, from the fear of going beyond the confines of the known, the familiar, the predictable and genuinely reaching out to the mystery of being, the mystery of being ourselves, the mystery of being more than our present selves, the mystery of being with others who are as much mystery as we are ourselves. From this side of that process, it looks frightening —as well it should. For from this side we really experience the existence of the nothingness beyond, as well we should, because there is as yet nothing there. It is here, on this side, that we can and do experience something of the terror of death, of not being any longer. And unless we are one of those stoic souls who can screw their courage to the sticking point and walk through fire, we need someone who can make the passage easy, who can lead us into the emptiness beyond to fill it with life, spirit, history. For it is only to the extent that this kind of liberation has taken place that we can experience our life as history, *our* history, freely brought into being rather than a blind interaction of brute natural forces. And it is only to the extent that we can continue to go beyond our present experience, our present being to more being, more spirit, that we can call ourselves at all "true" to our own human reality. And this is the fidelity, the truth which makes us and will continue to make us free.

Hope. Finally, it is the unity in these three experiences, the experiences of consciousness, the experience of our own time, and our own freedom which grounds and brings about the experience of hope. Once again, what we mean by hope is not an abstract conviction; if the experience of hope is a reality, it is a real emotional and intellectual attitude which is based on real human experience. This runs completely counter to the rather dogmatic positions of both pessimism and optimism. In the name of what he calls "realism," the pessimist looks at the human situation and forecasts no change: no change from the observed brutality, selfishness, antagonisms which make up so much of past and present human history. All we can hope for is a continuation of human evil continually swallowing up whatever meager human efforts for human good we might manage to bring forth. The dogmatism of this attitude is based on the fact that since there have been so few bright spots in the history of man, there is no use expecting that we can or will do any better in the future. The opposite, but equally dogmatic attitude is that of the optimist. For the optimist, things will be better because they *must* be better. Myths of unlimited progress, technological, political or any other kind of utopia are expressions of the dogmatic attitude which Freud calls "illusion," the projected fulfillment of our deep wishes for the future. But both the pessimist and the optimist fail the truth of the human situation in that they posit a future which is, in a sense, already "out there," so that we are freed from the necessity of actively bringing *our* future into being. Instead we are told that *the* future will come into being by itself; all we have to do is sit back and things will take care of themselves—stuff will just happen.

Neither pessimism nor optimism are experiences of human hope. In fact, they are not experiences at all; they are positions which are previous to and compensate for the lack of human experience. And as such, they are the posturings of people who are in fact without hope. The experience of hope is quite different. Put in its starkest but most pregnant form, the experience of hope is found in the emotional and intellectual confidence which we have in our own being. And when we reflect on the meaning of "I am" which we have developed thus far, we can see that it is found in the confidence that it is and will remain meaningful and worthwhile to be human, in possession of our own existence, engaged in decision, risk, involvement and thus continually coming into possession of "our" time, "our" present, "our" future, continually finding ourselves liberated from the obstacles which keep us from really "being" in this active and growing sense. Our hope, then, is a confidence in being, in spirit, the "more" of being.

But what separates the hoping spirit from the hopelessness of the pessimist and the wishful thinking of the optimist is *experience*. And the experience which liberates our capacity for confidence in our own being, our own present and future is precisely the experience of liberation we have just considered. Real hope depends for its realism on those events which have liberated more and more our capacity to be spirit and all that spirit implies—of which hoping itself is an essential aspect. It is only to the extent that we have had the experience of being liberated from the sameness, the inevitability of our past and the past, that we can have any realistic confidence in our own capacity to be, to be spirit. Thus, the love of friends, the overcoming of personal paralyses, historical events of liberation, all these liberate in us the awareness and confidence that we have and therefore can influence and really own our personal or collective present and future. To be sure, we are and must be aware of our past and present weaknesses, fears, failures. But to the extent that these have been overcome, we have experienced and do experience liberation; things, we do not have to be the same; we can go beyond the limits of sameness, fear, failure and bring something new into being in our life, our world. And to the extent that we have not experienced these liberations, we can only resort to the masks of despair—indifference, pessimism or optimism. In other words, we feel freed from the rest of "nature," in the sense that our life is not locked into the ineluctable sequence of things as they have always happened; we are, we can be freed to be more, more than past, more than the present as a bland repetition of the past.

Hoping is a special experience of time, our own time. It faces the future, our future, but it faces the future out of a past and present which are experienced as our very own. In despair, past, present and future all belong to someone or something else —nature, repetitious history—even to a God who has it all already decided, already determined. But hoping in any realistic sense depends on our capacity to "take the past apart" and put it back together again out of the liberation we have experienced. We cannot simply dismiss our past—it lives on in who and how we are now, in the present. Without it we are really no one. Without it, we are catatonic—frozen, unable to be, to move. For better or for worse, we are who we have become in the way we have done or not done something about ourselves in the past. Thus, our awareness of who we are now includes a remembrance of who we have been, whence we have come. But the crucial question for real humanity is whether we can do anything about all this—our past and our present. Without any experience of freedom, we can only recall the past, summon up ghosts which haunt our present with the specter of an endless repetition of past events. But the experience of freedom gives us the capacity to literally re-member the past. Not simply to recall it, to summon up a series of decisions, successes, failures, but to unlock that series and put them back together again in a way which charges the presence of our awareness with new possibilities. In the words of N. O. Brown: dis-member—re-member. To recall the past as spirit is not to summon up ghosts. Rather it is to take that past apart out of the creative power of our own liberation and to re-assemble it in such a way that it contains the possibilities of a new and richer future. But, once again, we can only re-member the past in this creative way to the extent that we have experienced the liberation for humanity, for spirit. This gives us a new presence to ourselves—not the same old Joe, but someone who is full of *real* new possibilities. This is a new presence which can evoke a new faith in ourselves, in spirit, in more being—and that is real hope.

Thus the hoping spirit—really hoping and realistically hoping—is spirit liberated from the closed systems of either optimism or pessimism. And this spirit, if it is in fact really functioning as spirit, is at war with "flesh"—that part of us which prefers to settle for well-being rather than more being, which prefers the illusory security of the familiar past and the comfortable present. Every past experience can be dis-membered and re-membered. Every projection for the future is an open question, this precisely because of the fact that we have experienced the capacity to be freed from any necessity of being locked into any kind of necessary pattern. Thus our planning is tempered by our hoping; the imaging of our future is subject to the same dis-membering and re-membering as our recollection of the past. *This is of critical importance, because it is only in this experience of the genuine liberation of real hope that we can truly experience our own openness to the real mystery of our own being. It is only in this experience that we can experience that the history which our existence is, is truly fathomless, that the cry for more being which spirit is, is a cry for being which is absolutely open-ended, a constant open question.*

Of course, this is a far cry from the puerile omnipotence of the one whose optimism would maintain that everything is concretely possible for anyone who has the intestinal fortitude. Willing is not doing. This kind of optimism is really just one form of that dogmatic optimism which thinly masks an attitude of despair which tries to compensate for the absence of hope by the manufacturing of illusion. The desire to be the "super-man" is really wishful thinking which is created out of the frustration of hope rather than its fulfillment. Our *real* possibilities are very concrete, taking their departure from the actual place to which our freedom or lack of freedom have brought us in the real present. The point of our reflection here is not that we can do all, but that, to the extent that we experience ourselves as spirit, we can realistically experience our liberation from the patterns, successes and failures of the past and live into a future whose possibilities are always broader than the events of the past or the constrictions of the present. And because of this, our future is liberated from the despair of sameness and predictability. And in this sense we can actually experience the fact that our being is limitless, bottomless, a profound mystery.

Transcending Spirit

Thus, the experience of spirit (once again: to the extent that we really do experience ourselves as spirit) is an *experience of transcendence*. And this is the real point of this reflection up to this point. In the experience of transcendence, we do not experience some thing but we experience ourselves in a special spirit-ual way. Our experience of ourselves and our vision of our world is characterized by the liberating experience of ourselves as spirit. The ability to say "I am" in a spiritual way is a liberated and liberating affirmation of the freedom and mystery of our own being, of the open-ended nature of our history, and this, not as an abstract intellectual or systematic postulate, but as something which we *know* from a particular kind of experience. In the discontinuity from nature which we experience in consciousness, we can affirm out of our own experience that we are more than nature, not simply locked into the patterns of physical action and reaction. We can affirm that our existence is at least seminally our very own. In our experience of our own inner time, which makes *the* past, present and future into *our* past, present and future, we can affirm our transcendence over the brute forces of nature and history (mere chrono-logy) in the constant pattern of demand and response in which each moment can be the opportunity for the creation of a history which is uniquely *ours*. In our experience of freedom (real freedom, not mere abstract freedom) we experience our transcendence over the compulsion and despair of past performance; we experience the bursting of bonds, of limits and can really see and experience ourselves as freed to be, to be spirit, to be more, in a word, to be human. In the confidence which characterizes our experience of hope, we break through the limits of expectations and predictions with the confidence that no system can ever really close off our being, and we can call any system which tries to do so by its clear name: inhumanity.

Further, this experience of transcendence is critically important for what we call "religion" and "religious experience." There are all sorts of religions and religious experiences for sale in the market place of public opinion. Meditation, drugs, "natural" foods, fasting, continence—so many "guaranteed" paths to "transcendence." So often what is actually on sale is some way of escaping (= "transcending") the malaise of contemporary culture or existence. But the real human experience of transcendence is no escape. If it needed a slogan, that slogan might well be: no idols and no magic. It would insist that there is no "turn on" which gets us home free, nothing so "with it" that we can get "out of it." No idols. No magic. Only the on-going task of more being, more consciousness, more awareness of the challenge and opportunity of our own time, more freedom, more hope—only spirit, the "more" of our existence. Only the on-going struggle between the call of spirit for more being and the call of flesh for well-being. And a religion which attempts to peddle anything other than this process shared in spirit is simply peddling illusion, inhumanity.

Our Spirit

Up to this point, our reflection on our experience of spirit has dealt with our experience of ourselves. It has been a reflection on the meaning of what it means to really be able to say "I am" in a genuine confidence in the truth of our own being, in a genuine confidence in ourselves as spirit. We have reflected on the truth of our own being, at least in the sense that it is possible and hopefully experientially meaningful to be true to spirit, faithful to the task of becoming all that spirit reveals itself to be. But this is, at best, only half the picture. For spirit is not only an experience of what it means to be able to say, "I am," out of meaningful experience. It is also the capacity to say, "*We are*," out of the same kind of experiential conviction and confidence.

We have and use our capacity to say "we" in all sorts of ways; we are not alone in the world. The very fact that these pages have been written and are being read flows out of the consciousness that we share our condition of being human, of being spirit. We are aware of our having to do something about *our*selves, about *our* world. And of course, we do that something in all sorts of ways. If we experience ourselves as one with "nature" in the sense that we cannot escape the locked-in inevitabilities and predictabilities of things, we will see the rest of the human species as equally locked in, equally devoid of any really new possibilities. The Germans have a word for this. They call it *da*-sein—being *there*. And the "there" in question is that outside sort of place where we spend so many of our waking and even dreaming hours: the seven A.M. to the city, the papers, the tools, the people who consume our human energy, the brown bag or the three-martini lunch, the same old talk of business, sports, anything to pass the time, the five P.M. home, the usual squabble at the dinner table, the TV, maybe some love-making with more or less love, and the expectation of the same tomorrow and to-morrow and tomorrow. The Bible has a word for this, too. It is called "flesh," that aspect of ourselves which is simply con-tinuous with nature, predictable, mortal, that aspect in us which consumes the freedom of spirit and locks us into the unending patterns of *the* past, *the* present, *the* future, that aspect in us that neither has nor is question, but only the same old answer. The consciousness of this aspect of our humanity is unavoid-able. What makes the difference is a matter of spirit. It is a matter of the quality of our consciousness, our vision, our experience. And the locked-in man operates out of a vision in which everything, people included, is always the same. Around and around we go, hopeless, dead. From what has emerged from our consideration of the meaning of "spirit" it should be apparent that this kind of vision and experience of one's self and one's world is one in which spirit, rather than coming into its own, is constantly stifled and runs the risk of being so dominated by "flesh" that it effectively ceases to be spirit in any real sense of the word.

The basis for spirit's capacity to say, "We are," is found in a fairly common experience. We can express this experience simply by our consciousness that someone else is "there." This is an unavoidable aspect of human experience. And the "there" in question is the "there" which we have just described—the fact that our consciousness, our time, our freedom and our hopes are being and must be worked out in a day-to-day pattern, a pattern which both releases and confines us, makes us "be" in a more or less sort of way. We experience other people around us as sharing in this kind of being-there. It forms the background and much of the content of our communication with one another. We become aware of the fact that we share the same experience, the same vision of life with other people. And to the extent that we have this awareness, there emerges in our consciousness the possibility of a greater sharing of vision and experience. Thus, rather than experiencing other people as simply "out there" like the stones or the running brooks, we are aware of other people as having an "inside" to them like ourselves. Thus we can come to know and relate to them in a different way—"from the inside." We can share our "inside," our joy, our sorrow, our frustration, with people who have the same kind of an "inside." In other words, this shared condition contains an opening to an inter-subjectivity. What is important here is the fact that this opening, this possibility, to the extent that it is real and concrete, is *a matter of shared spirit*. It is a matter of a shared capacity to see, experience and act, which is at the very basis of the human condition. To the extent that this shared spirit is realized in a living functional way, communication and deeper sharing of vision and experience becomes more and more possible. And to the extent that it is not or cannot be realized, communication becomes more and more difficult, if not impossible. Why this communication is important will emerge when we reflect on the realization of this "we-experience."

The "we-experience" comes into being and operation to the extent that we experience a conscious and explicit being and acting with one another. This is a very fluid reality, admitting of all kinds of differences of degree and intensity. But, in general, it happens whenever we address ourselves in a conscious unity to some common project or endeavor. It may be just working together, building or maintaining some structure or enterprise. It may be on a deeper level, that of the sharing or propagation of ideas, vision, ideals. Or it may reach its depth when we love each other and become conscious of the fact that more and more of our life is a matter of "we" as one spirit compenetrates another and the two spirits literally "dwell" in one another. In love, we become more and more conscious of the fact that everything we are and do is a coexistence and a cooperation, even when those we love are not around to take an explicit part in our life and activity. They are "here" in a very real and active sense. What is important here is that this presence of someone else in our life and activity does not crowd our life and action. Quite to the contrary, it makes us and our activity more and more our own. Yet, paradoxically, we become aware more and more that to really be ourselves in the deepest and most solid sense of the words means to be with someone else who calls us to life in the experience of love. Put another way, our deepest capacity to say, "I am," depends paradoxically enough on the fact that there is someone else at our depth who is there saying, "You are." To be spirit means to be a fellow spirit. To be spirit is not just a matter of *my* consciousness, *my* vision, *my* time, *my* freedom, *my* hopes; rather it is a matter of *our* consciousness, *our* vision, *our* time, *our* freedom, *our* hopes.

This is absolutely critical for any real understanding of what it really means to be spirit, to be human. If spirit is a cry for more being, then it is a cry for shared being. More spirit is shared spirit and shared spirit is not diminished in the sharing but it is enlarged and deepened precisely in the sharing. Thus, the very humanity of being human depends on and can be gauged by our capacity to say, "We are," in a realized and functioning sense. To the extent that we cannot say this, we are less human. And this lack of our own humanity comes home to us in many ways. It is far easier for us, more suited to our contentment with "well-being" to blame the evils in our world, the wars, the violence, the crime on "them." "They" kill, starve, gas, burn, rob or rape one another. "We" have no part in it. Like Pharisees, we gather the spotless fringes of "our" spirit up lest we be sullied by contact with "them." Spotless and innocent as we may look to ourselves in all this, we ignore the fact that in this kind of projection, blaming and punishing, we render ourselves in fact less human. Maybe this is the most pragmatic way to go about it right now, but the fact is that if we think about it and ourselves, we cannot avoid the sad conclusion that spirit has a long way to go, no matter how far it has come to date. And as bad as others may look to us, we must sadly strike our own breasts and say that we share very much in the fleshy condition which blocks and locks in the expansive and explosive power of spirit, turning this free-moving principle from a fresh, refreshing breeze into just so much dead air. "Ask not for whom the bell tolls—it tolls for thee and me."

Thus, spirit, that dimension which is a constant cry in us for more being, reaches out not only into our future, but it also reaches out, practically infinitely, to the lateral dimensions of our present to say, "We are," in concert with the totality of spirit in our world. The more people we can gather into our "we," for better or for worse, for fulfillment or for judgment, the more spirit we are, the more human we are. The humanity of all that is human, the spirit of all that is spirit really belongs to the humanity and spirit of each one of us. And the inhumanity of all that is inhuman belongs to us, too, to each and every one of us.

From all our reflection up to this point it should be appar-

ent that when we talk about "spirit," we are not talking about
"spirit-in-general" or "any old spirit," but about the concrete
experience of spirit, the way spirit actually is, what it actually
has become. We are talking about a concrete, actively functioning principle, a concrete and active quality of our human vision,
experience and action right now. And when we look at spirit
in this way, we can see that it is full of liberating potentiality of
consciousness and of the dead, dull predictability of the unconscious. It is full of the excitement of a time which is our very
own, a time for decision, a time to be fashioned as our own and
also of the deadly and ineluctable reality of "father time,"
Chronos, whose movement is relentless and has no care for
spirit. "The moving finger writes . . ." It is a spirit full of freedom gained through transcendence and of un-freedom, the
legacy of our contentment in well-being. It is a spirit struggling
for hopefulness against hopelessness. It is a spirit which at
once calls out for the presence and even the intimacy of "we"
but also draws back from presence to cripple its own humanity
in splendid isolation. Thus it is that to the extent that we are
spirit, that we really have become spirit, we experience spirit
as a reality which must constantly be gained, constantly brought
into concrete existence as we move between the terror and the
liberation of the processes of transcendence. And in this light,
the deepest human (and the deepest religious) question is not
so much, "Who am I?" Rather, it should be, "Who will I be?"
How will I fill up my consciousness, my time? What will my
history, our history be? And the question reaches out as the
rest of spirit makes its claims on our consciousness, our time,
our freedom and our hopes: who will we be; what will our
time and history be?

Spirit and God

It is against this background of our reflection on the experience of our own being spirit that we can reflect on the
meaning of "God." Once again, the question is one of meaning,

the question of the reference *within* our experience which this word indicates. Once again, it is a question of the meaning of the "absolute" to the extent that this is revealed to us within the framework of our very relative experience. It is, in this sense, a historical question, a question of what emerges within our personal and corporate existence as spirit moving, to the extent that we really are spirit, to the constant enlargement of spirit, to more and more being. And as the question of our existence as historical spirit, it is a deeply personal question. It is not a question of man-in-general questioning himself in terms of some absolute-in-general. It is a question of what reality gives ground, density and light to *my* life, *our* life. This cannot be stressed too strongly because to the extent that we are asking a *real* question, we are questioning a concrete, historical existence, our very own existence. Thus, the question arises not from the fabled "abstract man in the state of nature" (which a professor once described as a philosophy major swimming in the nude), but from the real experience of real people.

As we have seen in our reflection on the theme of "God," the question of God is deeper than "Who will I/we be?" The practical question which faces us is, "Why be spirit at all, in any functioning sense of the word?" And the origin of the question is in the very relativity of our experience of ourselves as spirit in our world. And once again, this relativity is not an abstract quality, reasoned to by syllogism or learned even from books such as this. It is a relativity which is known deeply and personally in the challenging or dissolution of any or all of the idealized images of ourselves which form the basis for our vision and experience of the world and our action in it. It is a relativity which forms the more and more conscious context of our plans as, out of the necessity of constantly adjusting our images of ourselves and our future, we become more and more aware of their contingency. It is a relativity which becomes more and more the context of our freedom as, out of the experience of our own un-freedom, we become more and more aware of the limitation of our own autonomy. It is a relativity which more and more forms the context of our own temporality as, in the constant attempt to make our time our own, we feel the relentless burden of natural time and decay, thus experiencing the fact that our time is only more or less our own. And so the question arises over and over: "Who shall I be; Who shall we be; Why be at all?" And more and more we become aware of the fact that we *are* that question, that spirit is always in quest, in question. And the question continually prompts the questing —for more—more being, more spirit, more humanity. Spirit is an invitation to transcendence.

And as we have seen in our earlier reflection on "God," what emerges from this questing and this question is not a new object of vision or experience. Rather what we come to experience is a "new spirit"—a new and broader context, horizon or background for our vision, experience and action. This is the "object" of our questing and our question. What we find is a new perspective for integration of ourselves, our past, our world, our fellow spirits. The world, ourselves, our fellow human beings light up from the inside and for the first time, perhaps, we really can see, see nothing new, but everything in a new way. And this new capacity, this new background for vision and experience is not just a new theoretical framework for interpreting the world. It is a whole new context out of which we can *live* in the world. For we see ourselves and our world out of a whole new quality of consciousness, liberated from the deadly repetition of the past. We see that we can truly take hold of time and make it our own. And all of this liberates within us the amazing hope that being, spirit, humanity —all this is, after all, really possible. The degree to which all this can take place, depends, of course, on just how much spirit we really have become. It may be a matter of "Uh huh, I see." Or "*Wow!* Do you see what I see?" Or all the flags are flying and everyone is singing, "Oh say, can you *see?*" What depth this gives to Flip Wilson's coy remark, "What you *see* is what you get!" It's all a matter of spirit.

What emerges, then, from the process of the transcending

spirit is *absolute spirit*. Not absolute "ghost," however, not a
shape or an object, but an absolute ground, an absolute horizon,
an absolute background against which we can not only state
but deeply confess that humanity, that spirit is absolutely
possible. All we can experience direct-ly or object-ively is a
deepening of what it is to be conscious, a liberation of a
seemingly unshakeable hope. But precisely *in* and *through* this
experience a *living* God is partially revealed. And what is important to stress over and over again is the fact that no new
object is revealed. What is revealed is a whole new depth of
reality and possibility of everything that is and is seen. Some
would say that the living God is revealed as the "other side" of
these experiences, just as one side of a coin always contains
and reveals by indirection the other side. It seems preferable,
however, in the context of what has been seen in our reflection
on the reality of spirit that it would be better to speak of this
revelation as always taking place on "this side" of our vision.
What is revealed is not seen, but is rather a seeing eye in us, a
reality behind our vision and experience of everything, a reality
which gives new depth, new solidity to everything because It
gives new depth and solidity to our capacity to see, to our
spirit.

Thus, as the background for the deeply personal and historical reality of spirit, there is gradually revealed the reality of
a *living* God. This God is a far cry from the detached script-
writer God of deism (and of much religion since deism). This
is not the God who wound history up in the beginning and
allows it to tick its way to the end where either with a bang or
a whimper it all comes out the way it was put together in the
first place. That kind of God is truly Lord of the dead, the
hopeless, the previously condemned or previously saved who,
in the last analysis, don't make any difference at all. The living
God is one who comes to be known as a part of our history, a
hidden part, it is true, but a part nonetheless. As we enter into
and pass through the experiences of transcendence, we gain an
ever greater confidence in the goodness, the value of our very

personal and historical existence. The liberation of hope gives us and our personal history more and more substance, more and more depth and solidity. The possibility of truly existing in an active and growing way increases; we become more and more possible. Rather than being hemmed in by the stale predictabilities of past performance, our lives become deeper and deeper until their possibility and challenge becomes practically fathomless. And it is in and through this experience that we hear, perhaps quite faintly at first but with increasing clarity a "voice" which calls us into active functioning existence at an ever deepening place in our lives. It is a voice which says a simple enough word, "Thou," speaking us into reality and existence. But that "Thou" is not a static word which simply puts us "there." It is rather a clearer and clearer command, the first commandment, "Thou shalt be! More and More thou shalt be!" A faceless hidden Ground is discovered when we reflect that our lives have become more and more possible and we face our future with the growing confidence that this is an irrevocable commandment which grounds our experience of the promise which our lives become.

Here, then, there is revealed a "true God," but not in the sense that this hidden and deeply mysterious presence corresponds to some abstract concept of "God." Rather, it is a God who is true to the call, the command which calls into being, a living and true God whose reality is discovered as the reality of *promise,* the promise to be there always, with us, *Emmanuel.* And it is this truth which, as it is discovered within our experience, grounds and activates our truth, our being true to our own existence so that we not only know the truth of ourselves, but we enter into the process of *doing* our existence in spirit and in truth. Thus the living, the true God is not a distant abstract principle, but is a God infinitely close, intimate beyond description to the fabric of our consciousness, our time, our freedom and our hope. This is a God of history, whose infinity is known as the possibilities of existence enlarge their perimeters into the limitless possibilities of the future.

And, at the same time, this is a God whose face is truly hidden as every concrete possibility opens beyond itself into ever new horizons, ever new possibilities for our lives and history. Hidden, yes; absent, by no means!

Thus, to the extent that we can become more and more spirit, more and more human, more and more our real selves, there emerges within our experience an ever receding horizon for our own possibility. The structure and limits of existence become more and more open-ended, and there is revealed an absolute—an absolutely open-ended background against which we can always be more, be someone new in possibility, new in reality. Every image shatters before the reality of such a God. Every idol crumbles and falls to the extent that we follow after this Absolute Spirit, the Spirit which calls our spirit constantly into new being. This is not an old God, but a new God, ever new and fresh, ever young in revelation of the absolutely new which reaches out before us. And the land of His promise is not a place of sedentary comfort, filled with the stable sanctuaries of fat idols. This is truly a God of Exodus, calling on us to follow after to a land which is always new, always yet to be gained. As His Spirit takes over more and more of our spirit, makes us more and more spirit, old men have new dreams and young men have new visions opening up new summonses to a new life.

In the last analysis, then, it is really all a matter of *spirit*. Man, God, history, religion are all a matter of spirit. To the extent that these realities come into active historical existence, they come into experiential operation within the horizons of spirit. They are known for what they are to the extent that we develop a capacity to *see,* a capacity for vision which is characterized by an ever-deepening concrete consciousness, by a more and more serious awareness of our own time, by more and more liberation from the dead dreams of the past and an opening to the limitless possibilities of the future, by a more and more concrete hope in the deep possibility of our future. They are experienced as real to the extent that we can experience ourselves, our fellow spirits and our world out of the context of more and more spirit, more and more consciousness, liberation and hope. And they actually come into concrete existence to the extent that spirit can act as spirit, out of this same deepening of consciousness, liberation and hope. Without this consciousness, this capacity to see, experience and act, man, God, history, religion can only remain idle dreams for the optimist, cruel illusions for the pessimist, opiates for the comfortable, illusions for the desperate. God can only become God, the living God, the true God, Emmanuel, God truly with us, to the extent that spirit becomes more and more spirit and we really come to *see*. And rather than negating or trivializing the human, the living God is the background against which the human becomes precisely more human. In this context, the god of any kind of deism goes finally and permanently to his grave, and we can begin in earnest to search for a living experience of a living God.

Thus the reality of God, the living God is a matter of spirit, indeed a matter of *shared spirit*. God only becomes a true God, a living God to the extent that we allow our spirit, our horizon for vision, experience and action to be overtaken by the limitless possibilities of an Absolute Spirit. Only then can our vision, our consciousness, our freedom, our hope come to operate against a background which is seen and experienced as limitless. Only then can that Infinity come into operation in our world through the channel of our limited, but ever expanding and deepening vision, experience and action. Once again, it is all a matter of spirit, of our spirit becoming more and more spirit against the background and horizon of absolute, infinite spirit as this is revealed within our experience of spirit, revealing ever new horizons for our own being spirit.

Spirit and Sacrament

The question of meaning, the search for some experiential referent for the language we use to express our religious experience, cuts through many temptations to pretension in the practice of religion. However, this cutting process, although it cuts us to the very quick, is not fatal. It reveals the fact that religion can be realistic, if it will keep human experience constantly in its focus. Over and over again, the question of meaning must be asked. And this question, far from being some form of bored agnosticism is in reality a call for a living experience of a living God. It forces many of our idols to the ground, forces us to be more honest and less pretentious about ourselves and what we have in our possession. Paradoxically, it asks us to lose "God" in order to find God. And this questioning and reflection has some clear implications for the practice of sacramental religion.

There is an old dictum in sacramental theology which says, *Sacramenta sunt propter homines* (sacraments are for men). God doesn't need them to be Himself, but we do need them to express and deepen our relationship with the deep mystery which pervades our being and history. As we will see when we come to an explicit reflection on the theme of "sacrament," sacraments are expressions of the process of being spirit and a deepening of that achievement in the very expression of it. They are, in a more traditional language, signs and causes of spirit, this in a very particular way. They celebrate the processes of consciousness, time, freedom, hope and human fellowship in spirit and seek to promote the progress of these realities in human life—all of this so that the reality of the living God can emerge more and more within the horizons of human experience. For the reality of the gift which we call "grace" only comes about to the extent that we follow after this mystery in our lives and experience and allow it to take more and more possession of our reality as spirit. Thus, in questioning the meaning of sacramental religion, we must take the old dictum seriously—this is all for man. This reflection has been a search for the meaning of man—what it means to be man, what the experience of truly being and becoming human involves. And it has been a search for the meaning of "God" within the horizon of human experience. Searching our experience honestly, we come to see that nothing can cause a relationship between ourselves and our God except our own fidelity to the depths of what it really means to be human. It's all a matter of spirit, our spirit being opened to and opening itself to the depths of our very human existence and entering into the process of becoming more and more human, more and more spirit. This is what religion and sacrament are all about.

The first effect of this reflection is to eliminate any possibility of "magic" at the very outset of the consideration of sacraments in human life. What is "magic" after all, if not the projection of our human transcendence onto some exterior principle in the hope that that exterior principle will accomplish what only we can accomplish—human transcendence, human spirit, human existence. Magic tries to get hold of a god by the tail and manipulate the god into doing things for us. Some people probably still believe that this kind of god still runs the weather and sundry natural phenomena. Most of us don't. But there are probably many who trust in sacraments to achieve what we can only achieve by our own faith, hope and love—the process of becoming human. No ritual, no sacred language, no matter how evocative or threatening can do that for us. The reality of the living God and our commitment to Him can only take place within the framework of our becoming more and more human in spirit and in truth. These are symbolic actions, which, if they have any power at all, have that power in their truth: the truth of humanity which we bring to them, the truth of God's hidden but all-pervasive self-revelation to us, the truth of our following after the living and true God in spirit and truth. Nothing can make up for this. Without this, they are simply false signs, sterile or pharisaical religious posturings which may make us feel very "religious," but which have little or no religious content. The power of sacraments, the power of this symbolic worship is a matter of spirit and truth. We will return to this consideration in a later reflection, but it is important to see that, at the very beginning, there is no magic.

A second implication for sacramental religion is the relativizing of sacrament which we considered briefly at the end of our first reflection on the theme "God." Sacraments, if we take them to mean ritual, instruments, elements, formulae, etc., are not holy of themselves. Whatever holiness there is, there is the holiness of the people and the God who becomes their God in the sharing of Spirit. Genuflections, bows, incense, reverence—these all have their place. But their value is completely secondary to the place where the deepest reverence belongs—to God and His image—the man who seeks to follow after God in spirit and in truth. Tradition is holy, but only to the extent that it serves to hand on what reveals God to man and relate man to God—spirit and truth. And in this light, the question of meaning must be directed to the ritual forms of sacramental religion over and over again—what does it mean? To the extent that we endow these human symbols, human formulations with the holiness of God, we are simply creating idols for ourselves and impeding the deepest reality of sacramental religion: man's relation to God in spirit and truth. The reluctance to permit this question and its practical answers to take place in the worshipping community betrays the presence of a spirit, all right, the vision, the experience and the action of the bureaucrat. For the bureaucrat, the basic vision is the fact that people really cannot handle freedom; it merely produces chaos. A good administration is better than the best constitution. So freedom is stifled in the name of order and the "general good." The question for today is whether we really can believe in spirit, whether we can in fact liberate the spirit we share for a new life, for more life.

Finally, religion has to do with letting God be God in our lives. This is the real, the existential worship we have to offer God. But the startling conclusion which emerges from the question of meaning and our reflection on spirit is that in a very real and functional sense God can *be more or less God*. And this more and less really depends on us. Our reverence for and service of God consist in a deep sense in letting God

be more and more God as His Spirit takes over more and more
of our world through our vision, our experience, our action.
This is important for the Christological reflection which follows.
But it has a profound effect on our own religious attitude. For
it opens up the meaning of "God" to the question of God's
future as our God. And our religious concern is no longer the
search for the one who is fully God so that we can bow down
before Him. Rather, our religious concern centers on the
reality of our own life as the place where God becomes God
more and more, hopefully until the day when God is fully God,
all in all. The question is no longer simply "Who is God?" The
question which engages our lives, our spirit, our truth is "Who
will God be?"

The Christ

Our approach to some understanding of the mystery of Jesus, the Christ, departs, once again, from the question of meaning, from the question of human experience and which human experience is contained in or promoted by the vision and practice of Christianity. This is a challenging, a demanding question. It demands that Christians come out from behind religious language, swinging or splendiferous liturgical demonstration and tell themselves and the world what all this has to do with the ordinary fabric of their own or anyone else's life. For it does no good to speak of Jesus as the Lord, the Man for Others, the Hope of Humanity unless it is clear within the Christian's experience and demonstrable to human experience in general that this dominating Person really means something valuable in terms of our experience of ourselves and our world, unless it is clear beyond doubt that the Christ's and the Christian's service of the world is in fact a service to the world and not simply self-serving, self-justifying, unless this vision and service do in fact liberate man's hope in and for humanity in such a living experiential way that we can truly see new and exciting possibilities for the very process of being human. Thus, our concern in this reflection is for the meaning of Jesus and of Christianity and this not in some closed sense for the comfort of the belonging believer but rather in the broader sense of the

meaningfulness of the Christian message for any human being
—and thus for ourselves in the depth and breadth of our own
humanity.

The Risen Lord

The focus of this reflection is a man, Jesus of Nazareth. But
this man is not a man like other men. True, he lived, he walked,
he talked like other men of his time. But the experience of this
man is unique. Some see him as the definitive center of their
experience of and faith in God. Others see him as a great man,
a good man, even a religious prophet on a par with the great
prophetic figures of Judaism or Islam. Today, he is variously
seen as a model for the revolutionary, the way back to meaning for the disillusioned young, the alcoholic, the drug addict.
A hundred years ago philosophers and theologians, skeptical
of the simplistic or even superstitious piety of the believers,
tried to come up with the "real Jesus," the historical figure
revealed in the writings of the New Testament. Applying the
canons of historical research and criticism of their time, they
arrived either at a perfect model of the Victorian gentleman
or, in their more skeptical mood, a fiction created out of religious and/or psychological illusion. Just about everyone agrees
that this man actually lived and the skeptics of a hundred or so
years ago who deny this fact are seen for what they were,
operating out of a point of view which could not tolerate the
phenomenon of Jesus or of Christianity because of the incom-
patability of either of these with the full functioning of the
"enlightened man." Some people still think this way, but no
serious historian could dispute the fact that this man lived and
died at a time sufficiently documented by historical record. So
the question of Jesus of Nazareth is not a question of historical
fact. It is a question of meaning: "What does this man mean?"
We might even suppose that if some of the recording opportu-
nities which we have today were available at that time, tape

recorders, filming equipment, etc., these might furnish us with a far more accurate and perhaps interesting short but eventful (or maybe not so eventful) life of Jesus of Nazareth, son of Joseph and Mary. But even such a detailed record of that life and that death would only give us a picture of a man like other men, even the other religious leaders of his time: a carpenter's son, later a rabbi, eventually executed for treason or blasphemy. But there were many others like him at the time, challenging the Jewish establishment, the Roman forces of occupation. And they ended like him, executed by crucifixion.

But it is there, with his death, that the similarity with other men ends. True, his followers experienced the same bitter disappointment that the followers of the other religious and political leaders of that period experienced. Any hope of the re-establishment of the Jewish monarchy and Jewish independence was nailed to the cross with him, buried with him. But within a short time, a different message was heard from his students and followers: he is not dead, he is alive and what is more, he is the anointed one of God through whom the long-awaited kingdom of God has become a new and earth-shaking reality. The example of this early preaching which we find in the book of the Acts of the Apostles gives us a specimen of this startling message: "This Jesus God has raised up, and we are all witnesses of this . . . and so let all the house of Israel know with absolute certainty that God has made him both Lord and Christ—this Jesus whom you crucified" (2:32, 36). It's a whole new ball game: God—one; everyone else—zero. But that *one* is a score so sure that it means the whole rest of the game. It changes everything and it changes it for good. So the thing to do is to change the whole set of your mind, your vision and join those of us who see this, by being baptized in the name of Jesus, the anointed one, and this will bring you the forgiveness of your sins and the gift of the Holy Spirit (2:37–38). And this spirit, this vision, is not just for a chosen few—it is for everyone, Jews, Parthians, Medes, Elamites, Mesapotamians and so on (2:9). The spirit, the vision, the great new thing is for everyone, just as Joel said a few hundred years ago. It's the end and a whole new beginning and the beginning has happened because God has raised Jesus of Nazareth from the dead, made him the anointed one of God and Lord of the kingdom in which God rules over everyone and everything.

Thus, the meaning of Jesus was experienced through the experience of Jesus as alive, as the Lord, as the Christ, the anointed one of God. And these experiences are not just casually connected with one another. They are all aspects of one another. There were and are other stories of people being raised from the dead. They are startling stories and make people wonder what is going on when dead people come out of their graves or get up from their death bed. But, as far as we know, they all end up eventually dead again. Not so with Jesus. His followers saw that Jesus was alive, but alive in a completely new and different way. It is far more than a matter of "Guess who I saw on the way to Emmaus the other day?" The experience in which Jesus is known to be alive reaches far deeper than curiosity or even amazement. It reaches into the depths of the lives of those who see him and says something utterly new to and about their lives, their world. Rather than experience like "Wow! there's Jesus; I thought that they killed him a few days ago," this experience would be something like "Wow! I'm a whole new thing; the world, history is all different, because I have seen that Jesus is alive and he is the Lord!" And along with this, there is the experience that one must tell this great good news to everyone—"Wow! Do you see what I see? Jesus is alive, God is really King now, and everything, everyone is different!" The way in which Jesus is alive has everything to do with the way we are alive and will be alive. It has everything to say about whether we are alive at all.

Of course, we are accustomed to a far more sober proclamation of this event. Its focus lays more emphasis on the divinity of Jesus understood more in the ontological categories of the Greco-Roman foundations of our culture. The resurrection is the great demonstration of this divinity. Consequently, Jesus can be adored (in the strict sense!) just like God. But this has far more practical implications. It means that the gospel of and about Jesus as it is proclaimed by the Christian church is a divine revelation, which has the authority to bind men's minds and consciences just as if God Himself could be seen and heard. In its more bizarre and simplistic forms, this understanding of Jesus as risen from the dead uses its divine origins to sanction almost every aspect of its very human accomplishments—after all, it's all a matter of divine foundation, divine law, divine right. The resurrection of Jesus proves that everything that the Christian Church does and says is right. Of course, all this owes its origin more to the developments of medieval, Renaissance and counter-Reformation theologies of the church, but certainly one aspect of the possibility of this kind of development has been the emphasis and insistence on the divinity of Jesus as a distinct but integral part of his "person."

The origins of this kind of emphasis are to be found in the inevitable passage of the original Christian experience from the thought-world of Judaism to that of the Hellenistic world of the New Testament times themselves. As the earlier New Testament documents look back from the experience of the resurrection to the life and deeds of Jesus, they speak in the language of the expectations of Judaism fulfilled in this man. Thus, they refer to Jesus out of a tradition of eschatological titles which describe the one who is to come and establish the reign of God over all men and all of history. He is called "Son of Man" in the tradition of the late apocalyptic of the Book of Daniel, "Son of God" in the language of the Psalms, "the Lord" perhaps from the liturgical life of the earliest Christian community as it reflected the liturgical life of Israel in prayer and song. But by the time the gospel of John is written, there is a new emphasis on the unique quality of Jesus' relation to God.

Over and over he is simply called "the Son." And the use of
the title certainly reflects the Jewish idea of a son as one who
in his thought, speech and action faithfully mirrors the image
of his father. John uses this title and its implied relation to the
Father as an antiphonal theme running through the whole of
the gospel and found in almost every chapter. The Son does
what he is commanded, he speaks what he has heard, he can
do nothing except what he has been commanded, his very
food is to the will of the Father. It is more a moral and existential name for Jesus. But already in the thought world of Greek-
speaking and thinking Christians, this name has a more
ontological overtone, that of one who is equal in nature to the
Father, equally divine, equally eternal. And consequently we
find in the prologue as elsewhere in the gospel itself statements
of the eternity of this unique sonship, from the beginning of
the world itself. Whether or not John himself thought or wrote
in the more abstract categories of Greek thought is still de-
bated by scholars in New Testament studies and studies of
primitive Christian Christology. But it is clear that by the third
century, the developing Christology was busily engaged in
threading its way between the two extremes of so emphasizing
the distinct divinity of Jesus that one ends up with three gods
(tritheism) and so emphasizing the unity of Jesus with God
that one loses the distinction between them (modalism). This
struggle for expression found its culmination in the formulation
of the council of Chalcedon (A.D. 451) in which the Christological formula which has become theological and doctrinal
tradition for over fifteen hundred years was finally hammered
out: Jesus, the Lord, the only-begotten Son of God is equal to
God in divinity, equal to us in humanity, truly human, truly
divine and yet not two persons; at the depth of His reality the
human and divine are united without the human becoming
divine or the divine becoming human. Thus, God remains God
and man remains man, but in Jesus there is a deep existential
unity between the divine and human, a unity which has come
to be called "hypostatic unity." And it is in this framework,

that of a two-nature–one-person model that the understanding of Jesus has been searched out and preached for a millenium and a half.

But the question which faces us in these reflections is not the question of historical research and interpretation. It is the question of meaning. What does the statement that this one man, Jesus, is truly human and truly divine mean? And, once again, this is not an abstract question addressed to new concepts. It is a concrete question addressed to human experience. And, as such, it is addressed not only to the formula of Chalcedon and the theologies which followed on it. It is also addressed to the eschatological titles given to Jesus in the New Testament. What was and what is the experience which all this language brings to expression? What does any or all of this mean in terms of what we do or should experience which makes us not merely state nonchalantly that "Jesus is truly human and truly divine" but confess from a depth within us and our experience that "Jesus is my Lord, the Lord"? Thus, the question of meaning cuts across the formulae of centuries to ask the same religious question of the New Testament and of the councils and theologians of every age of Christianity. What does it all mean? What difference does it make?

The first answer that should be made to the question of meaning is that both the New Testament titles given to Jesus, Lord, the Christ, and so forth, and the more philosophical statements about divine and human nature in hypostatic unity *mean the same thing*. Historically, this is apparent from the continued concern of councils and theologians for an identity between their formulations and those of the New Testament. Their constant concern was, "Are we saying the same thing in our formulations that the New Testament is saying in its formulations?" To the extent that their formulations said the same thing, they were retained, preached and defended. To the extent that new formulations contradicted what the New Testament said about Jesus, with due allowance for the translation into another framework for thinking and speaking, they were re-

jected as inconsistent with Christian experience and faith. This
may be a simple point to make, but it is of the greatest importance for us when we ask the question of meaning. For it
means that we are on the same quest, asking the same question
as the New Testament, the early councils and the whole history
of doctrine and theology has been forced to ask, "What does
our faith-expression mean? What is the underlying experience
which seeks to surface in these faith-formulae?" And it also
asks, "How can we formulate our experience of Jesus in a way
which means something to the experience of the world in which
we live?" And we are thus faced with a two-directional question, the question of the meaning of our present religious
language (thus, the question of preaching, teaching, sacraments) and the question of whether any contemporary formulation of our belief in this man, Jesus, *means the same thing*
as Christian faith from the beginning. Do we believe, in a word,
in the same Jesus? Granted that our world and our experience
of it and of ourselves may be different, does our profession and
proclamation of this man mean the same thing it has always
meant? And, once again, the question of meaning is obviously
not a question of language alone. Rather, it is a question of
experience: "Do we experience the same Jesus the New Testament witnesses and writers experienced, do we experience the
same Jesus the fourth and the thirteenth centuries experienced,
is Jesus, the Christ, truly the same yesterday and today?"

Further, the question of meaning and the quest for meaningfulness in language and practice asks whether our religious
language and practice are capable of conveying the experience
we have to the people of our time as well as deepening the
experience within ourselves. For the question of meaning in
Christianity is not simply the question of a private meaning
to be shared among initiates. The Christian experience, as will
emerge from this consideration, is not only an experience of
personal consciousness, liberation and hope—and interpretation
of ourselves and our world. The Christian experience is also
the experience of a calling, a calling to share this experience,

this in order that Jesus may be more and more Lord, that God may be more and more the God of men. The Christian experience is, then, the experience of a calling to change the world, change the people of the world to people with a new consciousness, a new liberation, a new hope. It is thus the experience of being called to live and act in a way that proclaims the truth and meaning of Jesus, the risen Lord, as the central meaning of humanity and our human history. And this is not simply a matter of words and formulae. It is a matter of the whole pattern of lives lived in such a way that the meaning of Jesus is conveyed in such a way that men become more human, more liberated to hope in the very future of man. It is a matter of the sharing of a new human spirit liberated and re-created in the Spirit of the risen Jesus. It is true that sacramental life looks more to the interior of the Christian community and seeks to strengthen and deepen the experience of the risen Lord for the Christian community itself. But the ultimate function of this deepening and strengthening of faith is that the Christian community function as a leaven for the hopes of the world.

Thus, the question of meaning drives us back to experience. And the first experience which we must search out is the experience of those who first made the startling proclamation that Jesus is alive, that Jesus is the Christ, the Lord. There are a number of reasons why we must return to that experience. First, that experience is the one against which every age of Christianity has sounded its expression to test its identity. But further, from what has emerged from our consideration on the themes of God and Spirit, we can see that there are serious problems today—problems of meaning and meaningfulness—with the mere repetition of the ancient formula of the hypostatic unity of divine and human nature in the one Jesus. There is not much of a problem with the human Jesus; indeed, today's revolutionaries find him a suitable and relevant model for our times. The problem of meaning arises with the difference of Jesus from the rest of us—a difference which the New Testament states in the titles "Lord" and "Christ" and which later doctrine and theology expresses by "divine nature." For the uniqueness of Jesus lies in His being a unique self-revelation of God. Some teaching and preaching has simply handled every mysterious aspect of the meaning of Jesus by adding the dimension of the divine to the human. The union of these two dimensions in Jesus makes Him unique indeed. His humanity is far more perfect than ours, he is sinless because a divine person cannot sin, his freedom is a very strange one (as is the "Father" who decides that Jesus is to be killed), he has the beatific vision, special infused knowledge, and some even go as far as teaching that Jesus was the greatest philosopher, theologian, artist, mathematician—after all, he is in the last analysis divine. It is as if "divine nature" is a reality which can be placed alongside "human nature" and the unity produces a man with special divine prerogatives who can do special "divine" things—like healing the sick, raising the dead and saving the sinner. But our reflection on the meaning and content of "God" has shown us that we cannot handle the "divine" in this way. The reality of the "divine" is not something which is known and conceptualized in the same way we know and conceptualize the rest of our human experience. And consequently it cannot be simply set alongside the experience of something which is different but the same to the extent that we have some concept of it and can use it in the same way we use the conceptualizations of our human experience. In this case, one and one do not make two at all, because the one and the one are so completely and undefinably different that they simply cannot be added to one another to form any kind of composition. In a word, the problem of meaning when we address it to the model of the unity of the divine and human in Jesus is that we know more or less what we mean by the human, but we have no possibility of conceptualizing the divine except to the extent that this reality reveals itself slowly and very personally within the processes of transcendence. And as such, it is a very different kind of knowledge and a conceptualization whose content is so deeply open ended that it can be said, in a very real sense, to have no content at all. We simply have no conclusive or inclusive idea of what it means to be God.

Thus, it is not quite fair to look at the accounts of the first experience of the risen Jesus and expect to find there a clear manifestation of someone or something which is "divine" in any of the comprehensive clarity to which at least, for better or for worse, Western theology and preaching has become accustomed. The accounts of the experience of the risen Jesus are to be taken literally, but their literal intention is by no means to speak in terms of the historical categories of the modern experience. They are written as Paul tells us "out of faith" and addressed "to faith" (Rom 1:17) and already presuppose a shared experience of the risen Lord which make them intelligible to the reader and aim at deepening and strengthening the vision of faith. They form a history, but it is a proclaimed and preached history rather than a mere matter of fact account of "what really happened." And thus our access to the experience which they contain and convey is rendered difficult if we try to interpret them by twentieth-century canons of historical interpretation. There is, in N. O. Brown's expression, a real "dis-membering" in order to "re-member" the experience. The details of the experience are taken apart and put back together in a new way in which the primary focus is the unique and strange experience of the fact that Jesus is alive and that Jesus is the Lord.

Thus, it should be no surprise that we find considerable dissimilarity when we try to find out "what really happened." As far as the event of Jesus' being raised from the dead itself is concerned, no account tells us what happened, and, in all probability, no account could tell us what actually happened. For this is a mystery hidden in inexpressible life and action of God. As far as the details of Jesus' appearance to the disciples are concerned, two traditions emerge rather clearly from the accounts. Luke and John situate the appearances of Jesus in Jerusalem, while Matthew situates this appearance in Galilee. The first ending of Mark's gospel doesn't even mention an appearance to the disciples, only an appearance to the women who ran away trembling with fear. Later an addition to Mark's gospel includes aspects of John's account (the appearance to Mary Magdalen) and Luke's account (the appearance to two disciples on the road and the appearance in the supper room). An addition to John's gospel, chapter twenty-one, includes Matthew's account of a Galilee appearance, but this time at the Lake of Tiberias rather than on the "high mountain" (an episode which in Matthew is loaded with the imagery of the third chapter of Exodus, with Jesus pronouncing His divine name, just as Jahwe did on Hermon: I will be there with you.) But running through all these differences there is one unmistakably clear statement and proclamation: Jesus has been raised from the dead and He is the Lord, the Christ. This is the central confession in the earliest of all the accounts of the appearances of Jesus after the resurrection, that of Paul in I Corinthians 15. There one can already see a highly stylized (and different) presentation of a series of appearances—to Peter, the twelve, the five hundred, James and finally (last or latest?) to Paul himself. But this whole tradition is brought to bear to illustrate the central fact of the tradition and its preaching—that the resurrection of Jesus is the faith in which we stand, and in which we are saved.

However, Paul brings out another point which is of the utmost importance for this reflection. And this is the fact that the knowledge that Jesus is risen, is the Lord, the Christ, is not something which is known by the mere repetition of a tradition and the testimony of witnesses. For the risen Jesus is not an idly noted historical fact. The knowledge of the risen Jesus is far more, a knowledge which reaches far deeper into one's life than a random fact of information. As Paul notes, ". . . no one can say Jesus is Lord except in the holy Spirit" (I Cor 12:3). And in terms of what has emerged from our reflection on the meaning of spirit, we can see that this confession is more than the simple statement of historical fact or event. The confession that Jesus is alive, that Jesus is the

Lord, the Christ arises from a deep change in a person's vision and experience of himself and his world. And this is an absolutely essential aspect of the answer to the question of what happened in the event of the resurrection of Jesus.

We are accustomed to imagine what happened in the resurrection out of the framework of the liturgical tradition which celebrates this event as one of a series of events which are spread out over a fifty-day period. This is one tradition, the tradition of the book of the Acts of the Apostles which presents the resurrection taking place on the third day, the ascension/glorification of Jesus taking place forty days later and the event of Pentecost, the outpouring of the Holy Spirit taking place ten days later. The gospel of Luke presents a different tradition, however. There (c. 24) it is all a matter of a day: the appearance to the women, the disbelief of the apostles, the event on the road to Emmaus, the appearance in a supper room, the walk to Bethany and the departure of Jesus with the apostles returning to Jerusalem filled with joy and blessing. Thus, the ascension and the outpouring of the Spirit are more closely united into the events of one day. John's gospel brings them into an even closer unity. John presents the crucifixion as the "hour" in which Jesus is "raised up." It is there that the whole work of God in Jesus is brought to its consummation and fulfillment (the blood, the water, the unbroken bones) and the final act of Jesus on the cross is quite explicit: he bowed his head and handed over the spirit (19:30). The account of Acts has its own theological point to make: the witness of the apostles to the risen Jesus who was with them for forty days, the outpouring of the Spirit on the great harvest feast of Pentecost as God gathers in those who believe by the gift of the Spirit; the fact that the glorification of Jesus, the sending of the Spirit and the final fulfillment are the acts of God accomplished in God's own time (a fact of great importance as the end of the world failed to materialize). But all the accounts have the same basic point to make, the same message to convey: That Jesus, who lived and died, is the risen Lord, the Christ, and that in his resurrection the Spirit of God has been poured out into human history to give us the capacity to see that Jesus is the Lord, the Christ, and to give us the mission and charge to share this vision with the whole world.

Thus, when we ask the question of what happened in the event of the resurrection, we are in search of a human experience. We have no access at all to the human experience of Jesus, to what happened to Him in the resurrection. Paul tries to describe his experience of what Jesus was like when Paul saw Him, but he can only speak in contradictions. Jesus is not perishable, but imperishable; He is not dishonorable or weak, but glorious and strong; He is not physical but spiritual; He is not so much a living being as a life-giving Spirit. All we can gather from this is that a profound and total change took place in Jesus so that this man is known and experienced in a completely different way. As Jesus passed through the experience of death, He entered into a totally new way of being, a totally new way of human relationship to the reality of God and this is seen and reflected in the way He is known by men. It is a deeply mysterious and challenging figure which confronts the one who "sees" Him. For the vision of Jesus is not a physical event, but an event of spirit. And as such, it effects, challenges and changes the spirit of man, creating a new vision, a new experience and calling for a new pattern of action—a whole new creation. And, as an event of spirit, the "seeing" of Jesus is difficult, if not impossible to objectify. Jesus is not just "there" to be looked at in some physical way, the way we look at the other things and persons we see. Rather, His appearance is a life-giving and life-demanding event which challenges us to the depths of our existence. Perhaps an example will help illustrate what is meant here. A few years ago, a professor in his course on the Eucharist finished his lecture on the risen Jesus and the characteristics of the risen humanity of Jesus. He asked if there were any questions. One of the students, a self-professed "hard-headed realist" raised his hand and in a deliberate Florida drawl asked the professor, "What happened to the fish and the honeycomb?" "What fish and honeycomb?" "Why, the fish and honeycomb our Lord ate when He walked in through the doors in the supper room. Either it got glorified or it stuck to the walls when He walked out!" This is one way of trying to understand what happened in the resurrection and it has a name: physicism, the attempt to understand an event by reducing it to its physical details. This kind of questioning has a very limited purview and ignores the fact that the resurrection accounts are not this kind of physical history and even if they were, the meaning of the resurrection is not found in this kind of physical analysis. What emerges from all the attempts to describe the risen Jesus is the fact that Jesus is alive, He is "with God" in a way which makes it clear to those who experience His presence that Jesus is the Lord, the Christ, the one on whom God has poured out His Spirit. We can extend this consideration and say that this event of Spirit is at the core of the resurrection. For Jesus, this is an entrance into a transcendently different human experience of God, of Himself, of the world. And, as an event of Spirit, it contains a totally and radically different kind of vision, experience and action. And it is this unimaginable difference in His whole human experience which later and different modes of thought seek to express in the formulation of the "hypostatic unity." But perhaps the principal focus to keep before our minds is the fact that all this is, for Jesus, a *human* experience, transcendently different, but human nonetheless.

When we ask the question of what happened with reference to the first witness to the fact of the resurrection, we are plagued by the same kind of inaccessibility to physical fact and detail. The dissimilarities we have considered make a reconstruction of the event very difficult and some commentators state quite blandly that all the accounts probably treat one and the same experience reconstructed in different ways to bring out different aspects of its meaning. But several elements emerge even from these differences. One is that Jesus is not known like any other object or person. He is not "there to be seen" and then seen. This is certainly part of the significance of the story about Mary Magdalen and about the happening on the road to Emmaus. Jesus is only really "seen" when He takes the initiative in self-communication—a word of tenderness, the breaking of the bread. It is in these ways that Jesus takes the initiative and renders Himself really and effectively present in that initiative. Thus, it is not a matter of physical detail, putting hands in wounds or the like. It is a matter of a self-communication, the communication of a spirit. And this is certainly consistent with the appearance of Jesus as Paul describes it (Acts 9:1–9; 22:4–16; 26:9–18; Gal 1:13–17). Coupled with Paul's description of the resurrection of other people, the only paradigm of which is Paul's experience of the risen Jesus, this description of the appearance of the risen Jesus is not an event in which Jesus enters someone's field of vision; rather the appearance itself gives the person the capacity to see. It is a self-communication of Jesus, but this self-communication involves and is mediated by a communication of a spirit.

Another element which emerges from these accounts is that the vision of the risen Jesus brings about a profound change in those who see Him. This change is variously described as a great joy which comes over them, they praise and bless God. For those who lived with Jesus, there is an experience of a great fulfillment of all of God's promises as is evidenced in the examples of preaching by Peter and Stephen. They are filled with such confidence that not even death shakes it. For Paul, the experience so changed his focus that he had to go off into the desert to reassess his whole life. And from this point of view, the main thrust of the resurrection accounts not so much what happened to Jesus. That is there to some extent, but the principle focus of the accounts is what happens to those who "see Jesus." The vision of the risen Jesus is a profoundly moving event which brings about a whole new way of seeing everything else, man, God, history. And this change is not only a personal change. It carries with it the drive to go out and share the experience, the vision with anyone who will listen and even with those who will not listen. It is an experience to be shared with everyone, Jew, Greek, Parthian, Mede, everyone. And the radical novelty of this new vision, this new spirit, is manifested in the startling signs which accompany a new revelation of God. But in this revelation, instead of the sun going dark, the moon turning to blood, the stars falling and all the sheep dying, there is an ecstatic outpouring of joy, peace, wonder. The confession that Jesus is Lord comes from a spirit profoundly renewed in joy, wonder and hope. Of course, all the descriptions of the outpouring of this spirit are not equally literal in their descriptions. In Corinth, for example, there is a great deal of ecstasy and ecstatic speech, ecstatic preaching inspiring ecstatic faith and so on. But, as the rest of the letters to the Corinthians show, it is far from a complete transformation of everything base and degrading in man; there are still divisions, scandals, fanatic enthusiasms. And one can look with a somewhat jaundiced eye on the nostalgic descriptions of early Christian life in the beginnings of the book of Acts, the possession of everything in common, the selling of everything to assist the poor, the joyous community meals, the universal favor they found with all people (Acts 2:43–47). There was probably much more to it than that. But the point of these descriptions and recollections is still clear: the experience of the resurrection is an experience of a profound change of spirit, a profound change of vision, experience and action.

Thus, the question of what happened in the resurrection is not so much a question of what happened to Jesus. The real meaning and impact of the experience of the resurrection is what happens to us, to those who are given the eyes to see the risen Jesus. And here again we are driven back to the recognition that this is a matter of spirit—a matter of a capacity to see, experience and act in a wholly new way. What our vision and experience center on is not so much one object among other objects in a field of vision as a focus, a horizon in which and against which everything else is seen and experienced in a completely new and profoundly changed way. The gospels point this out to some extent when they speak of the joy of the disciples *viso domino* (when they "saw the Lord"). But Paul spells it out in much more detail as he outlines the effect of this new spirit. For the believer, this capacity for vision and experience becomes *the* Spirit, the spirit of God, of Jesus. This vision and experience becomes a pledge, the first experience which is the beginning of a whole new way of seeing and experience, an experience which contains within it the promise of a deepened and expanded life which makes ordinary living look like death by comparison. This vision, this experience of one's self and one's world is the beginning of our own being raised from the death which life in the "mortal body" really is (Rom 8:11). It is out of this new vision and experience that we come to know that we are free-born (*liberi*) of God— that we are liberated from the lethal processes of unredeemed "nature" to pursue the emerging value and meaningfulness of human existence, a pursuit which is grounded in the unshakable confidence that human existence is good, very good. No matter what the obstacles which hinder or conceal this object of our confidence (the sufferings of the present, the future, hidden or apparent dominating powers, etc.), we can press on in our confidence and in this process we slowly gain the "glorious liberty of the children (*liberi*) of God," our adoption as sons, the redemption of our bodies (*ibid.* 12 ff.).

Paul pursues the experience further in both its personal and its cosmic significance. In personal terms, the gaining and sharing of this Spirit takes place within the context of a life whose quality is manifested and determined by the "fruits" of this quality of vision and experience: love, joy, peace, patience with one another, kindness to one another, goodness to one another, faithfulness to one another, gentleness with one another and self-control (Gal 5:22–23). When we compare these with the works of the "mortal body" (general licentiousness and carousing, enmity, strife, jealousy, anger, selfishness, dissension, party spirit), we can see that this vision arises from an experience of human life which creates and binds the human community together rather than fragmenting it, casting its members adrift to make do for themselves. This vision arises from the human experience of community which reenforces from within human experience itself the confidence that human existence is possible, valuable, worthwhile. In more cosmic terms, Paul indicates that this spirit, this vision and experience against which one experiences one's self and one's whole world, gives a whole new meaning to history. Now history is seen as a positive and gracious possibility, loaded with grace and blessing. Now the "eyes of our hearts are given the light to see the hope to which we are called, the glorious inheritance which is ours" (Eph 1:3–23). And the pledge and seal of all this new depth and solidity given to human history itself is the fact that now we are "sealed" by the "Holy Spirit," the fact that this new capacity to see reveals a new meaning to our personal and corporate human history which is all summed up in one confession: Jesus is the Lord. The letter to the Hebrews brings this out when it indicates the incompleteness of any history without its fulfillment in the lives of Christians today. It speaks of the great faith and accomplishments of the kings, patriarchs and prophets, it speaks of their hard lives—stoned, sawn in two, killed by the sword, wandering around in the skins of sheep and goats, over deserts and mountains, dwelling in the dens and caves of the earth. But, the author adds, their lives were incomplete, no matter how heroic they were, because God had foreseen something better for *us,* that apart from *us* they should not be made perfect (11:32–40). The point is that it is our lives now, our vision, our experience, our action which are moving the world to its completion. And we might add that even Jesus is not perfected apart from us, as Paul points out quite explicitly. For it is in us that Jesus is constantly becoming the Christ, that the depth and meaning of history are being realized and revealed in that realization, that Jesus fills out the fullness of what it means to be Lord, Christ and we fill it out in and for Him (Eph 4:11–16).

Thus, it is out of this personal experience and cosmic vision that there erupts from within human experience not an abstract theological or doctrinal statement but a living profession, confession, JESUS IS THE LORD! to the glory of God.

What emerges from this reflection is our awareness that Easter is Pentecost and Pentecost is Easter. These two mysteries represent two dimensions of one and the same reality, capable, it is true, of distinction, but inseparable from one another if we are to really understand the meaning of either one. What all this means is that the resurrection of Jesus from the dead is radically *for us*. But this "for us" character of the resurrection has its reality precisely in the coming of spirit, the spirit of God, the spirit of Jesus which forms a whole new context and background of the whole of our human experience. And it is only out of this new experiential context that we can say with any real meaning at all that Jesus is alive. For it is more than an idle statement about a new piece of information when we say that Jesus is alive. For while this profession says something about Jesus, it says this only out of the framework of a change in our vision and our experience and thus says much more that is meaningful about us. And this dimension of meaning is precisely the reality of spirit, of Pentecost. Thus, when we confess that Jesus is alive, we are confessing that He is alive *for us*—this is the basic meaningfulness of the resurrection faith. It is the same with the confession that Jesus is Lord. For the Lordship which we confess has its meaningfulness in the context of our understanding and living of our personal and corporate history. It is a confession of radically new possibilities for history as the reality of God emerges in a new way within human consciousness, freedom and hope. In other words, it is a confession that the spirit of God has given a new depth and solidity to human history. But the focus out of which this new depth and solidity emerge is the focus of our vision, our experience, our action as the spirit of God bears witness in, to and through our spirit to the new creation of utterly new possibility. So Jesus is Lord, but He is *my* Lord, *our* Lord in terms of my history, our history.

It is interesting to note, too, that this dimension of the meaning of the resurrection is a very important, if often ignored dimension of the later development of the two-nature Christology of the councils from Nicaea to Chalcedon. We have noted that there was a strong consciousness of the unity between what these councils struggled to achieve and the professions of the New Testament. Thus, through all the struggles to speak of the risen Jesus as Lord and Christ in the language of "nature" and "person" in a conscious continuity with the New Testament faith, the concern lies far deeper than the abstract philosophical problem of the meaning of "nature" and "person" and their application to the reality of Jesus. For one of the dimensions of that struggle is precisely the importance of the meaning of all of this for us. From Irenaeus' idea of the "exchange" of divinity and humanity (the profession that God became man so that man might be divinized) to the now classic statement of Gregory of Nazianzus "What is not assumed by the Word is not healed . . ." the concern was far deeper than the matter of semantics. The concern was precisely a concern for what the "divinity" of Christ means for us. Of course, the emphasis on Spirit is far different in those ages from the character of these reflections. At that time the emphasis lay more on the Spirit as inspirer of scripture and the more abstract problem of the nature of the procession of the Spirit in the life of the Trinity; this, at least until the divinity of the Spirit came into question after Chalcedon. But in the emphasis on the meaning of the divinity of Jesus we can see a more significant emphasis on Spirit as the meaningfulness of the risen Jesus for us. For this meaningfulness, the fact stressed by the "assumption of humanity" into the life, death and resurrection of Jesus, lies neither in the numerical identity of Jesus' humanity with ours, nor with the more abstract identity between Jesus and ourselves in the fact that all of us, Jesus included, are human. It is, rather, precisely a matter of Spirit. One and the same identical spirit is the Spirit of Jesus, the Spirit of God and the Spirit which bears witness in our spirit that we are God's children. To the extent that that one Spirit becomes the context, background, horizon of our life—our vision, our experience, our action—the resurrection of Jesus is meaningful for our lives; and this not in the abstract sense of our recollection of an event out of a dead and distant past. Rather, that event, the resurrection of Jesus, is meaningful because what happened in the resurrection of Jesus is *taking place in our lives and our experience now*.

In this way, we can get behind the symbolic expressions of the "coming of the Spirit," the "outpouring of the Spirit, the descent of the Spirit from heaven," the dove, the wind, the tongues of fire. These are significant symbols: the dove, the symbol of peace, of the fulfillment of God's promise in human life and history; the wind, which knows no boundaries, no limits, which moves freely and freshly beyond any limit; the apocalyptic fire, the judgment, the cleansing, the purification, burning away the apparent to reveal the hidden, the true reality. But out of the fulfillment, the freeing, the transformation come a new capacity to see, to experience, to act—in a word, to live. And it is out of this whole newness of life and its context that there erupts the startling and unheard-of confession: Jesus is alive, Jesus is Lord. For now we can live out of a whole new background, see everything against a wholly new horizon, experience everything and act out of a wholly new context— in a word, we have a new spirit. And in this way a whole new heaven and a new earth come into being, brought about through the new Spirit, the same Spirit which brooded over the first chaos and bore the life-giving word of God, "Let there be light." It's all new in the newness of a new Spirit. And it is in this newness that the radical novelty of the resurrection has its meaning in our lives. The old passes away and the new is born in us.

And from all this, we can see that when we speak of the Holy Spirit, we are speaking of the very meaningfulness of the resurrection in human life, the very immediacy of the reality of the risen Jesus to and for us. This is not the ghost of an ancient recollection but a living presence, the presence of Jesus, alive and dominant *within* our own experience. And that presence is *in this Spirit.* This cannot be stressed too strongly if we are to grasp the reality and meaning of the resurrection in other than an abstract (and ultimately insignificant) way. For it is only in and out of this spirit that we can say that Jesus is alive, that Jesus is Lord with any real meaning at all.

With the Father

The New Testament accounts have more to say about the resurrection of Jesus than His emergence from the tomb and the deep personal knowledge that He is alive and is the Lord. And this continuation of the resurrection event is thematized, particularly in the Acts of the Apostles by the event of the Ascension. This glorification of Jesus, "the return of Jesus to His Father," is expressed in the only way possible for the writer of Acts. And this is in terms of a symbolic image of the structure of the universe which commentators and theologians refer to as the "three-layer universe." The Jewish mind of the first century understood the universe as composed of three levels. The central level was that of earth, a flat table on which the drama of human history was played out. Below this was the abode of the dead, *sheol,* where people lived in some sort of shadowy existence, eventually awaiting some kind of general resurrection. Above the earth was, obviously, the sky, the firmament. Above the firmament were the waters of the heavens, the stars, the angels, etc. And at the heights of the heavens, in the heaven of heavens, was the abode of God. The details of the structure are not of importance here. What is of importance is the fact that this symbolic structure of the universe is the only framework in which the writers of that time could express the fact that Jesus was glorified by God, at "God's right hand." And it is in this framework that the writer of Acts expressed the end of the physical presence of Jesus among other men and His entrance into a whole new life with God. Luke's gospel is more reserved in its description of the departure of Jesus. Jesus merely walks with His disciples out to Bethany and parts from them while He blesses them (Lk 24:50–51). But even there, He promises them that they will be given power "from on high." And some manuscripts of Luke's gospel contain a mention of the fact that "He was taken up into heaven."

What these accounts contain is a completion of the resurrection accounts, a more explicit cosmological symbolism which affirms that Jesus is alive and that His life is with God and for God. And, in terms of the image of the universe which the author has, this can only be expressed in one way—Jesus ascended to where God is, to be with God in glory. Thus we find the upward movement of Jesus, the cloud (recalling the symbol of God's presence in the Exodus and in the Temple) taking Jesus from their view and the message of the angel promising that Jesus will come in glory, in the clouds of heaven. Thus we have a very concrete symbolism which thematizes quite clearly the new life and character of Jesus. But there is still one element missing. In the context of Acts it is the "power of the Holy Spirit" and in Luke, it is the coming of the "promise of the Father" and the being "clothed with power from on high." What is not yet present in the ascension accounts is the element of Spirit which brings this account, like that of the resurrection, to its completion. In the context of Luke, the disciples go to the temple and praise God in joy. In Acts, they return to the supper room. But the full impact of the meaning of these events is still lacking. It is only with the coming of the Spirit that a "power" overtakes them, driving them out of their security into the market place to share the experience and meaning of their deep and transforming knowledge that Jesus is alive, that He is the Lord. It is in this event, then, in the coming of the Spirit, that the full implication of Jesus' resurrection comes home to the first disciples. It is there that the meaning of all these accounts falls together in a practical experiential way. It is there, in the coming of this Spirit, what their vision becomes more than a rejoicing over Jesus' victory and lets them see that this has a deep significance for everyone and all time. And thus the first examples of preaching contain more than a mere witness to the resurrection and glorification of Jesus. For these events have a deep significance for all men: it is the beginning of the time of fulfillment, the "last days" in which all of God's promises for man and for history are to be fulfilled. They preach a whole new beginning to history, a beginning which inspires fear in their first hearers: "What shall we *do?*" It inspires fury in the religious establishment leading to imprisonment, punishment, death. What all this means is that in the very preaching of the resurrection and ascension of Jesus, those who hear are confronted by a new Spirit, invited to a new vision, a new experience. In other words, in the coming of and the confrontation by this Spirit, the meaning of these events, their practical existential meaningfulness and demands reveal themselves and make their demands on those who hear the preaching. And in this the pattern of events and meaning as this took place in the experience of the disciples repeats itself in the experience of those who see and hear them. Without this Spirit, the event and its preaching remain foreign to the human situation of both the disciples and those to whom they preached. And it is only in that Spirit that the events of the resurrection and glorification of Jesus enter into the depths of human experience to reveal themselves and work their power in a claim on the totality of human vision, experience and action which human life is. And it is the coming of that Spirit which makes the difference. For those who open themselves to that Spirit, there is the joy, the enthusiasm, the deep changes which bring this group together. For those who refuse the new Spirit, there is only the same old history, the religion of law, obligation and hopelessness. From the first, it is apparent that it is all a matter of spirit.

Thus, when we take into account the cosmological confines of the New Testament accounts and ask ourselves what this would

mean in a different understanding of the world and of the
"place" God has "in the world," we are faced with the same
problem of time and eternity, mystery and history which
formed the context for our reflection on God. We need not
simply throw out those symbolic forms in which those who first
experienced the resurrection and glorification of Jesus expressed
their experience and the faith it grounded. For those expressions embody the conviction that the new life of Jesus is with
God and for God. And they contain and convey one aspect of
the resurrection: that Jesus is alive and that He is Lord with
God and for God. So much for eternity and mystery. But that
is only one side of the reality. There still remains the question
of meaning, the question of Spirit. And here we can and should
re-symbolize the meaningfulness of these events in a slightly
different framework. And in the context of time and history, the
context of the meaningfulness of these events for us, we can
change the religious and theological geography somewhat to say
that for Jesus to rise to God is, at the same time, for Jesus to
"rise" to the depths of the human. For the meaningfulness of
the resurrection of Jesus, its spirit dimension is in the effect
which this mystery has on our history, our humanity. Here, it
is a question of what becomes of man, what becomes of our
history. It becomes a question of what this does to our consciousness of ourselves and our world, our experience of time
and history; it becomes a question of whether and how this
event frees us to be more fully what we should be, whether and
how this event liberates in us the capacity to hope in our own
future. Here, the resurrection means a profound transformation of the human, the emergence of a new ground, a new
solidity and depth of meaning for the human.

However, when we reflect on the meaning of this new depth
and solidity to human existence and the place in human experience where this new depth confronts one, we can see that this
is not simply a matter of the transformation of the present. Far
more, it is a transformation of the future of man, an expansion
of the possibilities for being human. For, although the resur-

rection and glorification of Jesus says a great deal to our present, it does so by revealing a whole new future for human existence. The confession that Jesus is alive, that Jesus is the Lord, the Christ speaks to the question of who we are, but it does this by way of telling us who we can be, will be. Thus, when we rearrange our theological geography to speak of Jesus' rising to the depths of humanity, we are speaking of a rising into the future of man, revealing and promising that newness of life and its possibilities to every man. It is against this background and in this context that the first witnesses to the resurrection experienced the living Jesus. All their preaching of their own experience is framed in these categories of the fulfillment of expectation and the opening up of a whole new future for those who will believe. It is out of this background and context that the titles which are given to Jesus derive their meaning: Lord, Christ, Son of God, Son of Man, Son of David. It is the startling discovery that Jesus has become all that these titles connote that leads to the first preaching. But that discovery is mediated and borne, as we have seen, by the meaning of all this for those witnesses themselves. For the discovery of who Jesus is filters through the experience of who we can be now, of who we will be in the newness of the new Spirit. And the practical experiential reality to which that preaching addresses itself is the question, "Who will we be?" And the practical experiential question of the meaningfulness of the risen Jesus addresses itself to the question of who Jesus will be: Will He be Lord? Will He be Christ? Will He be Son of God? All this *for us*. Thus, rather than glorying passively in what has happened to Jesus, those who know that Jesus is Lord are challenged deeply in the very fiber of their lives. A radically new possibility for human existence is revealed and out of this revelation arises the question, "Will it be so? Who will Jesus be? Who will you be?" And, in terms of the question of meaning, we can see that this revelation and this question constitute the human experiential meaning and meaningfulness of the risen Jesus.

The Inspired Memory

It is out of this context of meaningfulness, then, that the first Christian community remembered and preached Jesus. As evident and well known as this is, it is important that we recall it here in order to give a focus to what we mean by the "inspiration" of the scriptural accounts of the life, death and resurrection of Jesus. Here again, it is a matter of Spirit. But what does this mean? In a word, it means that the accounts of the life of Jesus, accounts which are "good news" to those who remember, preach and believe in Him, are written out of a vision, an experience of life and the world in which the experience which proclaims that Jesus is alive, that He is Lord forms the dominating focus. But here again, we must ask the question of meaning, the question of what experience lay behind the memory of Jesus which found its expression in the New Testament accounts of His life, death and resurrection as well as the accounts of His powerful presence as it was experienced in the first Christian community. And we must ask this question because we are faced with the same question today, the question of the experience of Jesus as Lord, as Christ which rises to expression in our own understanding of who Jesus, the Christ really is today.

Once again, the traditional presentation of the idea of "Biblical inspiration" has centered on the way in which God has sanctioned, by the influence of the Holy Spirit, the recollection of the life of Jesus as the scripture presents it. The principal problem is the problem of how the inspired authors were moved to write what they actually wrote. Where did the ideas, the details come from? Are they true or not? And the truth and validity of these ideas, these memories is rooted in a mode of divine inspiration which gives an absolute sanction to the words of scripture because they are, in the last analysis, the words of God. And in this way, the validity of scripture is given an indubitable divine foundation which gives us the capacity to place an absolute trust in it. But, given the perspective and question which motivate these reflections, we are driven back once again to the question of meaning, the question of experience. It is all very well to root the confidence we have in the fact that God is the breath of scripture's life, making it useful for teaching, correction and training in righteousness (2 Tim 3:16). But we must ask the question of the meaning of this divine breath and the power it has for any of these uses. And, with the whole of tradition, we can say that it is a matter of spirit. But in the light of our earlier reflections on God and on Spirit, we can see that what this means is that the birth, the development and the relevance of scripture is a matter of a quality of consciousness, a capacity to see and experience. And this brings us to the question of the *concrete* content of this spirit.

The New Testament accounts of the reality of Jesus are remembrances of the man, Jesus, who lived, died and rose from the dead. They are accounts of the life, death and resurrection of Jesus, who is known as the Lord, the Christ. And this rather obvious fact is of the utmost importance. For this memory is not a simple recollection of bare historical facts. Rather, it is a memory which has its focus in the fact of the resurrection as this was experienced by those who first came to believe in and preach the risen Jesus. Thus, who this man is and was is not constructed from the careful collation of the details of a normal human life. Instead, who Jesus is and was, the same Jesus, is known through the filter of the experience which grounded the proclamation that Jesus is the Lord, i.e., the experience of the resurrection. And, in this light, the events of the life of Jesus which lead up to and include His death are seen and reported as the prelude to the event which grounds this proclamation. Thus, it is the *risen* Jesus who was born in Bethlehem, got lost in the temple, preached in Galilee and Judea, died on a hillside outside Jerusalem. The memories of Jesus which belonged to those who walked with Him from the beginning of His preaching are selected and arranged to hint constantly at the mysterious person this man really is. His preaching transcends the law and establishment of Israel. His words bear an unique authority. They are startling words, scandalous words, healing words, words which even give life to the dead. His whole life is blessing, grace and challenge. And His death is presented with the imagery of the appearance and act of God: the sun is darkened, the veil of the temple is torn in two, the earth shakes, the dead rise. The death of a man gives rise to the awesome confession, "Truly this was the Son of God." (Mt 27:45 ff.)

What these accounts present is obviously not the type of carefully researched biography which we call a careful and factual history. It is a history, but it is the history of a man who is raised from the dead and is made the Lord, the Christ. And, as such, it can only be written out of that experience which makes this vision and this confession possible. Thus the details of the life of Jesus which are remembered by those who saw Him walk the earth, are now taken apart and reconstructed, dis-membered in order to re-member, by those who have the capacity to see Him as the risen Lord. And the man who emerges in these accounts is not simply a man like other men, but is the *Lord* Jesus, Jesus, the *Christ,* Jesus the Son, Son of God, Son of Man. Thus, the concrete memory of Jesus is a memory whose details are reconstructed out of the experience of the significance of the Risen Lord. In these terms, his past is prelude, prelude to the revelation of who He is in the experience of Him as Lord and Christ. And in this sense, we can see that this is an *inspired* memory. It is a memory which can only be put together by those who have that capacity for vision and experience which allows men to "see the Lord." In a word, it is a memory which is inspired by a very particular spirit, *the* Spirit. This Spirit is the Spirit of Jesus, because in the revelation of the risen Jesus and the gift of the capacity to know that Jesus is alive, that He is the Lord, this Spirit bears the meaningfulness of the man Jesus to those who experience His being alive and Lord, this in the very experience of being able to "see the Lord." And it is the Spirit of God at the same time, because this revelation of the living Lord reveals at the same time the deepest meaning of human existence itself. For, as we have noted, this revelation is not the appearance of another more or less interesting object to the field of normal vision. It is, rather, a revelation which takes place in terms of every man's question about the meaning of his own life, about the meaning and value of human history itself.

In this sense, then, we can speak meaningfully about the inspiration of these memories of Jesus. But it is far from the old picture of the bird or the angel whispering into someone's ear. Rather, it is a matter of an experience which creates a whole new capacity to see, a whole new horizon for vision and experience which sees everything differently rather than merely seeing different things. It is, in Teilhard's words, a matter of diaphany rather than epiphany. It is a matter of a power which is experienced too closely to ever be an object of vision itself. But in that power of vision and experience, as we have noted, everything else is changed, seen differently. Thus, the gospel message about Jesus has more to do with us than it does with Jesus, because the focus of these narratives is on the meaning of this man *for us*. And this is precisely the Pentecost dimension of the resurrection event. The *"pro nobis,"* the meaningfulness of all this for us, is precisely the dimension of spirit. And it is out of this dimension, this perspective that the meaning of Jesus' life, death and resurrection are remembered. But it cannot be stressed too strongly that "re-membering" is precisely that. It is a reconstitution of the recollection of Jesus in the light of the shattering, the enlightening, the hope-filled and deeply transforming experience which conveys the "good news" (in reality both "good" and "news") that Jesus is alive, that He is our Lord, the Lord. Thus, if we want to go behind such expressions as "Jesus is the man for others," we can see that this is a matter of Spirit: the Spirit of this man, Jesus, raised from the dead, gives us the capacity to see that He is indeed the Lord, that our personal and corporate history has taken on a new depth of meaning and possibility and that all of this is rooted in what we see has happened to Jesus in His being raised from the dead. The whole reality of the "for others" dimension of the life of Jesus, then and now, is a matter of

Spirit, the Spirit of Jesus, the Spirit of God. It is this vision, this experience which breathed new life into the first Christian community, breathed life into its memory of Jesus, breathed life into the written record of that memory.

In terms of our reflection on the reality of spirit, we can see even more specifically what this Spirit contains in concrete terms. Perhaps it would be best to speak of this Spirit in terms of its being a totally and transcendently *new* Spirit. And its shattering, enlightening, transforming and hope-filled character lies precisely in the revelation of a reality which is absolutely new as the experience out of which the confession that Jesus is alive, is Lord, arises overtook the first Christians. And this all took place within the structures and questions of the human existence of those who experienced it. Faced with the question of consciousness, the question of their own existence—what they were to do about themselves—they found in their vision of the risen Jesus that a whole new spectrum of possibilities opened out for them. Their old selves, old limitations, the old slavery to the same old dead expectations—all this died when Jesus died for them. What replaced it was the capacity to walk a new way, in a newness of their whole life (Rom 6:3–11). Formerly, their life was dominated by the minute observation of law, now they were subject to a new power, the new Spirit (Rom 7:6). Now, they could put off all the old ways because the whole of their vision and understanding were made new, and in this newness is the very image and likeness of God (Eph 4:23–24). And thus, in their experience of the resurrection, of being "in Christ" is a whole new beginning, a whole new creation (2 Cor 5:17). Truly, the old has passed away, everything is new (*ibid.*).

This newness of life and history pervades the whole human structure of those who experience the newness of the new Spirit. Their sense of time is changed, because a whole new beginning for time has been brought about in the experience of the risen Jesus. For time is now the time of fulfillment, the fulfillment of man, the fulfillment of history. Now, we live in

the "last days," the days when all God's promises will be fulfilled, but these days are the new days, the days of the new
Adam, the new beginning (Acts 2:17; I Cor 15:45). Now
time is truly *kairos, the* time, the right time, the opportune
time, the acceptable time—a time for decision, a time for action, a time for the emergence of the new. But the newness of
this whole new time of new possibility is experienced in the
liberation from the old, the old law, the old sin, the old death
(Rom 8:2 ff.). In the new Spirit, all creation has been set free
from the old slavery, the old pattern of death and corruption
and set on the path to freedom, the glorious freedom of God's
free-born children (Rom 8:12–25). In the new Spirit, we are
freed from the slavery which lives in terror because the new
Spirit makes clear to our spirit that we are God's free-born
one, His children. Thus, we are freed by the Spirit, freed by a
new and startling truth—that Jesus is the Son, the Lord (Jn
8:32, 36). In this way, then, out of a whole new context and
horizon of liberation by the Spirit of Jesus, the Spirit of God,
we can enter anew into life, to live in a new and fresh way
even in the midst of the ambiguities and even the anguish of
human existence, for we know that all our groaning is the pain
of labor in which the free-born children of God are being
brought forth and revealed (Rom 8:18–25). It is the new Spirit,
the new vision, the new experience of ourselves and of history
out of which the cry arises, "Jesus is the Lord." It is out of a
whole new consciousness, a whole new being, a whole new and
liberated experience of time grounding a totally new hope that
we come to know what it means to say that Jesus is indeed the
Lord. It is, in a word, a matter of a new Spirit.

It is out of this inspired perspective and inspired experience
that the first Christians remembered Jesus. And, as we have
noted, this memory is not a simple factual restatement of the
past. For memory is not simply an accumulation of past facts.
Memory is a creative power which sees the past in the light of
the *present,* present experience, present perspective. And in
this experience, the past is dis-membered, taken apart. But it is

also re-membered, put back together again in terms of the
meaning of the past as prelude to present experience. Thus, the
New Testament contains an inspired memory, a memory animated by a very particular Spirit, the Spirit of God, the Spirit
of Jesus which is known in and at the same time makes known
the fact that Jesus is the living Lord, that God is more truly
God in the Lordship of Jesus. But the context in which the
meaning of these statements emerges is that of the question of
human life itself—what can we be, what will we be? And this
question and concern find a whole new answer in the resurrection of Jesus from the dead. Now, God is the God who raised
Jesus from the dead. And with Paul, we re-member God as
the one who is known precisely in the fact that He gives life
to the dead, dead bodies, dead hopes, dead minds and hearts.
Thus the *living* God is the God who brings some answer to the
question of who we will be. And this takes place first and foremost in the fact that God raised Jesus from the dead and
made Him His Christ and our Lord.

The Meaning of the Christ

This brief reflection on the inspiration of the New Testament memory of Jesus may seem interesting, maybe even novel
(which it is not, in fact). But it has not been developed because
it is either interesting or novel. It has been developed because
we today are faced with the same question as the New Testament writers, the same question as theologians and bishops of
the early Christological councils. And that question is a question of meaning. The focus of this reflection is on a man, a
human being, Jesus. But He is a human being with a capital
difference. For the experience of this man as the living Lord
associates Him intimately and inseparably with our deepest
questing and questioning in our search for God. The New
Testament writers thematized the meaning of Jesus in terms
of their own experience, the experience of a national religion

which discovered and remembered God in terms of their own history. And they called Him Lord of God's kingdom because the experience of the resurrection made abundantly clear to them the fact that God, the God of promise, was now the God who fulfilled His promise in giving life to the dead. History opens up with the fulfillment of that promise and human life enters into incredibly rich new promise. They called Him the Christ, the anointed of God because in the experience of the resurrection there is at once the experience of a new Spirit which is poured out on Jesus, poured out on those who see Him alive, the same Spirit in the Christ and those who, in that same Spirit, now live in the Christ in a total newness of life, its possibilities, its future. The theologians and bishops of the great Christological councils faced the same problem. But their language is different, speaking as it does out of a different cultural and philosophical background. They call Jesus true man, fully man because His humanity tells all our humanity what it is to truly be human, i.e., redeemed in Christ. They call Him true God because this graced condition of man is God's own work. And they call Him truly one because it is in this man, raised from the dead, that God has created humanity anew.

But, like the fathers of the early councils, we are faced with a second question. And this is the question of identity. Is this Jesus whom we proclaim today the *same* Jesus who was proclaimed by those who first made the Spirit-rooted proclamation that Jesus is alive, that He is Lord, Christ? Traditionally, this question has been answered in terms of the unity of Christian tradition and, in some respects, in terms of apostolic succession. The same message has been preached and taught (not always a fortunate expression) from the beginning by those who receive the commission to preach it in an unbroken succession to apostolic ministry in the Christian community. This is an application in practice of Vincent of Lerins' principle for Christian doctrine: that which has always and everywhere been believed by everyone. It envisions the Christian message as something which is universally taught and accepted, handed on from age to age in unbroken continuity. As helpful as this principle may be for defining what the Christian community can or cannot say is its formulation of faith, it still does not answer the contemporary question of meaning. The contemporary question of meaning, as we have noted repeatedly, asks where this tradition of language and practice finds its sanction in ordinary human experience. And from this point of view, we can see, in the light of our reflections on the reality of spirit and the meaning of the resurrection of Jesus, that the identity of Jesus is an identity which is mediated by the one Spirit of Jesus. In a word, *we experience the same Jesus to the extent that we are possessed by the same Spirit:* the same Spirit which is the horizon for Jesus' own relation to His Father, the same Spirit which gave the first witnesses to the resurrection the capacity to "see the Lord." It is this one Spirit which is the bond between the Christ and the Christian, between Christian and Christian in any particular age of the life of the Christian community and between the different ages in that same life. "For in *one* Spirit we have all been baptized into one body . . . and all of us have drunk *one* Spirit" (I Cor 12:13). The one Jesus is the one Lord in the one Spirit. The one God is the one God in the one Spirit!

But, as we have noted in our reflection on spirit, this is not just a matter of any old spirit. This is a very concrete and particular background and horizon for vision, for experience, for the activity of living. And its concreteness and particularity reside precisely in the fact that this is the Spirit of the risen Jesus, a new horizon, a new vision, a new experience, which bears witness within our spirit, our horizon, our vision, our experience, conveying there the meaning to our human experience that Jesus is indeed raised from the dead, is Lord, to the Glory of God, His Father and our Father in that one Spirit. And all this means that Jesus is Lord, is Christ to the extent that we are overtaken by the same new horizon for living which overtook those who saw Jesus the risen Lord for the first time. And out of this horizon we experience the same liberation of a radically new hope for our own individual and corporate history. This is what it means concretely and experientially to believe that Jesus is the Lord, the Christ. Within our own experience we find ourselves anointed by the same Spirit which anointed Jesus and anointed his first witnesses. "Jesus, the Christ, the same yesterday and today, and the same forever" (Hebr 13:8). The same Lord, the same Christ in the same Spirit.

Even more concretely, this all means that our belief that Jesus is the Christ takes place within a particular experience of our consciousness, our time, our freedom, our hope and our common human condition. Our consciousness, as we have noted, faces us with the question which we are: What will we do about ourselves? What can we be? What will we be? When we are overtaken by the Spirit of the Risen Jesus, there is liberated in our consciousness a transcendently new capacity to see. We can be, we will be what Jesus is. And what Jesus is speaks to us not only of what we can and will be after the terribly final act of dying. It speaks of that, to be sure and tells us that our life is imperishable, that it opens up through death to a life so rich, so intense and total, that the life we live now is death by comparison. Our God, our absolute and ultimate value and reality, is the One who gives life to the dead! We will be more, far more than we ever dreamed we could be. But, in His Spirit, the risen Jesus speaks to far more than this distant future. He speaks to all the futures which face us at every moment of our lives. He speaks to what we shall be now in the day-to-day pattern of our lives. And He speaks quite concretely. He says that we shall be more now in a constantly growing love, a constantly deepening peace and joy and that these are the fruit of the patience, the kindness, the goodness and mutual fidelity, the gentleness and self-control which bind the human condition together and give integration and solidity to every center of human existence and energy. And all this is grounded in the conviction which at once grounds this kind of consciousness and deepens it, the conviction that God is *for us,* for us in the same Spirit in which Jesus is *for us* (Rom 8:31). And thus there is no power which can overcome this Spirit and its consciousness in us. What indeed can we be, shall we be? We can and shall be more, more deeply *human* in the Spirit of the risen Jesus.

It is out of this Spirit-animated consciousness, then, that we can experience our liberation and the reality of our own time as the place in our life where freedom constantly comes into bloom. For it is only out of this kind of consciousness that we can experience any liberation from the not-yet character of our own humanity. For the root of our evil is precisely in the fact that we are in fact not yet human. All the fear, the anger, the hatred, the division that separate man from man and man from himself bear eloquent witness to the fact that, as far as we may have come in our technical capacities, we still have a long way to go in the very basic art of being human. And it is precisely to this condition, the very incompleteness of our humanity that the Spirit of the risen Jesus, and the risen Jesus in that Spirit, and God in both address the living word of liberation. This man, the risen Jesus, through the Spirit which is His and ours, says to our humanity that it is possible, that it is worthwhile to be truly human in all that we are and all that we do.

But this liberation, a liberation which calls us to be more and more human, is a constant liberation of the radically *new* in our consciousness and our hopes. For the One who is revealed to us in His Spirit is One who transcends, *in His humanity,* any of the forms of humanity which we experience. He summons us to a future which He already is—with God, in a way of being human which functions in an identity in Spirit which far exceeds any of our capacities to be at one with ourselves or with one another. For in His Spirit He is one with God, His Father, in a oneness transcendently deeper and more intense than any oneness we can achieve within ourselves or with one another. But this oneness, a oneness which finds its affirmation in the word which resonates at the depths of His humanity, "You are my beloved Son," is not just for Jesus. In that same Spirit, even this deep personal integration and unity with the absolute ground of His and our existence, is *for us,* a mystery of unity with God and with Himself which we are called to share in that one Spirit. In that one Spirit all that Jesus has become is for us, to be shared with us in an ever-growing depth and solidity in our own humanity, within our spirit, our experience. And that Spirit, as it overtakes and permeates our vision, our experience, our action is the pledge of our liberation to be human as Jesus Himself is human. Thus, our liberation, to the extent that the Spirit of Jesus overtakes our spirit, is experienced as a liberation for a truly new human-ity—not for the same old story of fear, hatred, division, war or the inhuman and dehumanizing utopian ideologies which are manufactured out of such deep human frustration. Jesus is the New Man, the last Adam, but, in His Spirit, He is all of this for us. And to the extent that His Spirit truly becomes our Spirit, we can know that we are truly God's free-born ones, His children in whom His Love is pledged as victorious over every force which seeks to smother it. And in this way, to re-turn to a previous reflection, to the extent that we are able to confess, in Spirit and in truth, that Jesus is indeed the Lord, we can experience a constant invitation to transcendence, the transcendence of everything in us that impedes our own new humanity.

But once again, we must be concrete. The invitation to transcendence which the Spirit of Jesus is just that—an invita-tion. There is no automatic, no magic way for all this to come about. Our memory of the risen Jesus is not a vague, abstract memory of someone who was raised from the dead a long time ago. It is a memory of someone who is known as the Risen One *within our experience* and is thus a very concrete memory which finds its content in *who we have actually become.* It is here, in the actual historical liberation of our capacity to be free to become new men, that the confession that Jesus is the Lord is, in existential fact, true or not. Thus, the memory of Jesus is a memory of our own lives, lives freed in the seeds which

His Spirit sows within our experience. This is not a vague ancient promise, but a living pledge which liberates within us the conviction that we can indeed be human in the works of the Spirit of Jesus, the Spirit of the One who raised Jesus from the dead. And it is only out of this living pledge that our hope in humanity itself is in any sense realistically grounded. For the future of the new man only becomes possible, credible, to the extent that it has already begun *within our own experience of our own lives*. Without this living experiential pledge, all we have is some kind of dogmatic optimism.

Thus, in a very real sense, we can see that whether or not Jesus is Lord and Christ depends for its living and historical truth on who we have become, who we are becoming. This is a living memory constructed out of the actuality of our consciousness, our liberation, our own time and hopes. It is a living profession which rises from what we know from experience and no amount of projection or pretense can give it its inner truth. For this is a truth which is *done,* not just discussed.

Jesus, the Sacrament

Finally, it is against this background that we can begin to think and speak meaningfully about Jesus as the basic *sacramental* reality. For *the* problem of sacramental theology today, as well as for every other branch of theology, is precisely the problem of meaning. Sacraments are, after all, symbolic acts, acts in which a meaning is brought to expression and deepened in the very act of expression. There has been a rediscovery of this dimension of the mystery of Jesus, the Christ. Out of the research of the Tübingen school in the early nineteenth century, there began to emerge a new consciousness of this ancient patristic theme, a theme carried on and enlarged recently in the explosion of sacramental theoretical writing since the 1950s. However, what has been lacking, both theoretically and practically, has been the dimension of Spirit as the bond between

God and Jesus, Jesus and Church, Church and sacramental
life. True, the reality of the Spirit has been there verbally as
well as in the theology which influenced the documents on the
Church and the liturgy from Vatican II. But the current question of meaning is not answered by the mere repetition of an
old and venerable tradition. Hence our insistence on the reflection of the meaning of spirit within human experience, man's
experience of himself, of God, of Jesus as the Christ.

The word "sacrament" comes from the Latin word *sacramentum,* which is a translation of the New Testament Greek
word *musterion.* Both these words have secular meanings, referring to oaths, the rituals and secret teachings of the many
cults which flourished in Greco-Roman civilization. But the
meaning which this word takes on in its Christian context is
that of a hidden, unseen reality which becomes visible and
tangible in a concrete historical event or person. That hidden
reality is, of course, *the* hidden reality, the mystery of God and
His loving dealing with man within man's history. And, of
course, from the Christian experience, *the* visible way in
which God's love comes to deal with man is in Jesus, the Lord,
the Christ. Paul finally elaborates this in his sweeping vision of
the whole of human history culminating in the fullness of
Christ—that God's secret plan and wish is that all of history
will find its fulfillment when everyone and everything finds its
unity, its meaning and its solidity in the man Jesus—"recapitu-
lated" in the Christ (Eph 1:10).

Thus, it is in Jesus that the full meaning of history is
brought to our vision and understanding so that our lives,
lived in the anointing with which Jesus was anointed, in His
Spirit, become the "praise of God's glory" (*ibid.,* 11–12). And
the pledge, the guarantee that this is in fact true is in the fact
that we have been "sealed with the promised Holy Spirit"
(v. 13). And the function of this Spirit within our spirit is to
charge our lives and talents with the power and the unity
which "builds up the body of the Christ" until it reaches its
full stature (4:11–14). It is in this way that human history

comes to its fulfillment, because in this way the mystery which was hidden for ages is now revealed—*the* secret now made visible which is the fact that the Christ is in you! (Col 2:27).

Thus, when we speak of Jesus as the basic sacramental reality, we are speaking of a man, Jesus of Nazareth, a man in whom the fullness of God's love for man is finally made historically visible and available to human experience. But it is absolutely essential to realize that when we speak of the man Jesus, we are speaking of the man who was raised from the dead and who is the Lord, the Christ, anointed in His resurrection by the Spirit of God in such a way that His very being man takes on a whole new meaning. For, in that Spirit, Jesus is one with God and one with us, for God and for us, in God and in us. The earliest level of Christian faith did not appreciate this. It placed Jesus in the heavens, at the right hand of God, seated in glory. He has triumphed and pretty soon God will come to end history and we will be glorified with Jesus. But the delay of this event caused a deepening of understanding of the reality of Jesus. It did not take Paul too long or too much disappointment to realize that the meaning of Jesus was far richer than this kind of expectation. And by the end of his ministry, we find this deep realization of the cosmic significance of Jesus emphasized so strongly. Far from losing its significance and value, history takes on a far deeper meaning and value. God will not be fully God, all in all, until Jesus becomes fully the Christ, fully anointed in the fullness of His humanity, our humanity. The physicism of a later theology lost sight of the strong realism of Paul's vision and came to speak of those who are one in this Spirit as the "mystical Body of Christ," a term borrowed from the medieval name for the Eucharist and elaborated in the ecclesiology of the late Middle Ages, the Renaissance and Counter-Reformation in a highly moralistic and juridical sense. It is only recently that theology and teaching have recovered a sense of the strong realism of Paul's (and John's) insistence on the reality of the presence of Jesus in the Christian, a presence which grounds a far more realistic

understanding of the "body of Christ." Thus, when we speak
of Jesus as the sacrament of God's presence and action in our
history, visible and tangible for human experience, we must
take most seriously the fact that we are speaking of the whole
Jesus, the whole Christ, a man who does not merely have the
breath of life, but who is indeed a life-giving Spirit, the Jesus
who is in God and in us, for God and for us—all this in the
one Spirit.

Thus, the sacramental reality of Jesus resides in His very humanity. But we must be aware of the uniqueness of this humanity
and its meaning for our own humanity. It is precisely in those
who are in Him in His Spirit that Jesus is the visible, tangible
form of the loving action of God in human history. Jesus is
the *Grundsakrament,* the basic, primal sacramental reality, but
He is this *in us.* The humanity of Jesus is, in Teilhard's words,
the divine milieu, the center for our humanness and the whole
context for human existence. And, as we have noted repeatedly,
this is all a matter of Spirit.

But, as the gospel warns us, it is not enough to say "Lord,
Lord." The Lordship of Jesus must be a reality, must have a
real meaning in our lives if we are to live in the Kingdom
(Mt 7:21–24). This brings us back once again to the question
of meaning: what does it mean to "Be in the Christ," to let
the reality of Jesus as Lord have meaning in our lives, our
experience? And, as we have seen, this is a matter of the
reality of the resurrection of Jesus forming the background,
the horizon for all our human vision, experience and action.
It is a matter of His Spirit overtaking and penetrating our spirit
to the extent that we can say that the reality of the risen Jesus
has compenetrated our whole selves. Jesus, the Christ, truly
lives, lives *in us.* We have reflected on the meaning of this in
our human experience. This Spirit is shared and communicated
among us through the fruits which it bears in the lives of those
who, even though they be bearers of the mystery of iniquity,
bear that Spirit as the background for the experience of their
lives. Scripture speaks of that Spirit as the Comforter, the

Spirit which strengthens us. But perhaps it would be better to
think of that Spirit as the Challenger, the Spirit which faces
our lives and summons us to more life, more vision. The
concrete fruits which this Spirit bears in the lives of those who
live out of this Spirit are a strengthening and empowering reality for us, but that Spirit communicated that strength for a purpose—to let our lives become dominated by Its revelation. For
what the Spirit reveals to us is the utterly new possibilities
which lie before us in the vision of the risen Jesus, who He has
become for us. Like the fire which is Its symbol, this Spirit
can penetrate to the very center of our lives and transform
everything we are and do from within, changing the most
ordinary aspects of our day-to-day existence with real life. It
calls us to life; It commands us to be. It calls us to a constant
newness of life; It commands us to be more. And to the extent
that we answer this summons of the Spirit, our lives reveal the
fact that Jesus *is* the Lord, the Christ. Our lives embody and
en-time that Easter/Pentecost event as a living historical reality. But they do this in a deeply human way, in the works of
love, joy, peace, patience, kindness, goodness, faithfulness,
gentleness, and self-control which make every aspect of our
lives, our work, our play more and more human.

It is in this very concrete, very human way, then, that
Jesus, the risen Lord is in fact *the* sacrament, the tangible
historical presence of God in our personal and corporate
human history. This may disappoint those who want Christ
and Christianity to stand for a particular ethic, a particular
social or political program. But neither the Christ nor Christianity have to do with any such system. Rather, the Christ and
Christianity speak to something far more profound which cuts
through the relativity of the ethics, social structures or political
systems of any age of human history. For the Christ and Christianity speak to the very humanness of the human, revealing it,
evoking it as we move through our history toward the fullness
of the human. Then, and only then, will Jesus be fully Lord,
God fully God, man fully man. Until that time, we are a pil-

grim race on the way to its true home. No holy empire, no holy war, no holy peace, only the constant struggle for the birth of the fully human. And it is in the name of that humanity which we seek that we can cry out against the inhuman and struggle to eliminate it from our midst.

The practical conclusion of this reflection on Jesus, the Christ, should be obvious. Briefly stated, it is this: the validity of Christianity as a symbol system depends on its capacity to share and evoke a *human experience*. The validity of any symbol system depends on its capacity to effectively convey the meaning which that symbol system is supposed to contain. If a symbol system fails to do this, it is invalid, perhaps not in the legalistic sense this word has come to possess, but it is invalid in the starkly simple sense that as a symbol system it just does not work. It is a melange of empty signs repeated perhaps out of duty or magical expectations, but in the last analysis conveying no real meaning, no real experience. It is pretense.

The meaning which the whole Christian symbol system is meant to convey is the total reality on which this reflection has centered: the experience that Jesus is alive, that He is the Lord. The life, structures, liturgy, every aspect of Christianity has to do with the handing on and sharing of a spirit, the Spirit; it has to do with the creation of an experienced background for our vision, experience and action out of which our transformed vision, experience and activity allow us to "see the Lord" in and through the transformed possibilities of our own lives. And the question of the validity of Christianity as a symbol system must be answered on this level—the level of the meaning which it evokes and deepens within our human experience. As long and as venerable as Christian tradition has been, it must ask itself this question in every age of its life. And if Christianity is to be faithful to the Christ, it must work in every age of its life to make its symbols meaningful in the sense that the whole context of Christian life will bear the Spirit which reveals the risen Jesus within our experience.

Against the background of this and the preceding reflections, we can see that a great deal, if not all the intelligibility and credibility of Christianity rest on the extent to which Christianity furthers and deepens the very reality of being human. Our own lack of humanity is at once the destruction of the credibility of the resurrrection and the judgment which history itself bears against us of being unfaithful to the charge which Jesus gives to us to preach the gospel to every nation. For in order to preach that gospel, that good news in any meaningful way at all, we must show in our own lives that that news is good news indeed and not just another religious system. In the last analysis, if God is to be God in any meaningful way, if Jesus is to be the Christ in any meaningful way, it will be because we are and are becoming more and more human. The most important religious thing that we can do is to be and become more and more human.

The Church
of the Christ

The meaning, the human experience of being a church, the church of the Christ is already apparent, to some extent, from our reflection on what it means within our own experience to say that Jesus is the Lord, the Christ. For the church of the Christ is God's creation, God's gathering together of a human community in human history; but it is this precisely in that Spirit which creates the vision and experience out of which we confess that Jesus is the Lord, the Christ. The church of the Christ is *ekklesia*, a community called together, gathered together by God. But, as we have seen, this is a matter of a shared spirit, a shared vision, a shared experience and a shared life whose center and context is the risen Jesus, with all this implies for our experience of ourselves, our world, our history. To be the Church of the Christ, then, means the experience of the liberation within our own lives to be and become more and more human, a process which bears within it the historical reality of Jesus' truly being Lord, of God's truly being God for us.

The Calling

Of course, at this time in the history of the church of the Christ, we would be less than frank if we ignored the fact that the experience of the resurrection of Jesus and the Pentecost event which this involves have a rather low visibility within the structures of established Christianity. We would be naive to ignore the fact that thousands upon thousands of people who have called themselves "Christian" find established Christianity meaningless, insignificant in terms of the needs of their human lives, and "vote with their feet," either publicly severing their connection with the organized churches or simply letting that connection wither away in a more quiet but equally effective way. But for those of us who continue our connection with the church community, this massive disaffection with Christianity must raise the question on which these reflections are centered: the question of meaning, the question of what the experience is which really does gather together a community of belief and life in the experience of the resurrection of Jesus and the Spirit which makes that experience possible and actual. Thus, unfortunate as this may be, our reflection will present more what the Church of the Christ *should be* rather than what it actually is. But this is important. For even in the face of the historical contention that every attempt at the reformation of the church since the middle ages has been a failure, we are never excused from the summons to reformation. *Ecclesia semper reformanda:* the church of the Christ always has been and always will be in constant need for reform. And the reason for this is easy to see. It lies in the fact that the Spirit of God, the Spirit of the Christ is borne and shared by people like ourselves, people in whom this Spirit is weakened and contradicted by another spirit, the spirit which summons us to well-being, to comfort, to self-service and self-justification rather than to more being, to the service and sanctification of all of God's world. And in this way, the question of reform always falls back on the most uncomfortable territory—that of ourselves, our own lives, our own vision, experience and action. But this is the only place where any real reform can begin. And thus, even if all too unhappily these reflections do not represent the actual experience which we have of the church of the Christ, they still must focus on who we should be, out of what spirit we should live, see, experience and act. Thus, as these reflections are written, it is with one hand on the keyboard and one busily engaged striking the breast. But it is hoped that these reflections will further the process of all prayerful reflection: the opening of one's life to that renewal which is the fruit of the new Spirit.

To be the church of the Christ, then, is a calling; it is a gathering. This is the theological principle behind the harvest significance of the opening narratives of the Acts of the Apostles. And this calling is brought about by means of a Spirit, the Spirit of God, the Spirit of the Christ. But, as we have noted, that Spirit brings about its work within our spirit, within the background for our own capacity to see and experience ourselves and our world, to act in our history. And what this Spirit gives us the capacity to see is the fact that Jesus is alive, is the Lord. But this "object" of our vision, the risen Jesus, is not seen as one object among other objects in our field of vision. Rather the risen Jesus is seen through the transformation which takes place within our own lives, within our vision of what it means to be human, of the possibility of being human in the transformation of our spirit, i.e., our consciousness of our selves and our own possibilities, our experience of what our time means, our liberation from the dead past to a new future, and, in all this, in the new hope which the risen Jesus reveals for our very humanity. This transformation of all that it means to be, to be in a truly human way, is the experience in which the Spirit of Jesus overtakes our lives, reveals the risen Jesus to us in a deeply personal and experiential way, and at the same time becomes the context out of which we see ourselves and our world as new, new in fact and new in possibility. But this is not all. Any transformation within our own experience, within our own lives has its effect not only on our attitude toward our "inner self," but it necessarily also effects our relations with our fellow human beings. It faces them with a changed person and demands a change at least in the way they will relate to us. We see this is the memory of those who first experienced in their lives that Jesus was raised from the dead. This experience brought about a deep change in their lives, but at the same time it drove them out to share their vision, their experience, the new Spirit with anyone who would listen. Their lives became an invitation to transcendence for everyone they met.

Thus, it is important to remember that the action by which God gathered in a harvest in the event of Pentecost is not merely the gathering together of a community which shares a secret kind of good news. Rather, this good news, the new Spirit is a news, a Spirit to be shared. Thus, the *ekklesia,* the calling and gathering which being the Church of the Christ means, is at the same time a sending, a driving of the Christian outside himself, outside the community of shared belief to tell the world that Jesus is risen from the dead, to ask the world of men whether they can see what we see. It is a gathering in the one Spirit, but it is also a mission to communicate that Spirit. And this communication takes place in many ways. We are accustomed to think first of all of verbal communication, books, pamphlets, sermons, the Hyde Park kind of defense of Christian faith. But the credibility of all this precedes the formalities of logic and lies first and foremost in the lives, the transformed lives of those who really *know* that Jesus is risen from the dead. For this knowledge at once grounds that quality of human existence which Paul describes when he enumerates the "fruits of the Spirit" and is deepened to the extent that these fruits blossom in our lives. And it is here, in love, in peace, joy, patience, understanding and so on, that the Spirit of the Christ is primarily shared and it is out of the context of this quality of life that our words about Jesus mean anything at all. Without this experience and quality of life, we have only another ideology.

This is a very important point to keep in mind. We have been accustomed to think of the church as a historical institution, founded by Jesus, which contains the grace of salvation for those who are within it. And this is true, at least in the affirmative sense. But Christians have moved all too easily from this affirmative understanding of the church to an exclusive understanding which in its classical formulation says that there is no salvation outside the church. Whatever this exclusive statement does mean (and it does not mean that people who are not Christian fail to find God or to live in the Spirit of the Christ), it does not mean that the church is simply a safe haven from the trials or burdens of human existence. Rather, it means that the church is a sacramental reality which means that like all sacramental realities, it is *propter homines,* "for man's sake," indeed for the sake of every human being. To be "church" is not simply for the sake of the Christian. It is a challenge, a charge to be and become more and more human for the sake of all humanity. Some people are shaken rather deeply by the clear consciousness within the teaching and preaching church by the insistence that the Spirit of God and the Christ is at work throughout the whole of the world, the universe. "If that is so, why be a Christian?" "What am I getting out of being a Christian?" In the light of our reflection on the meaning of the Christ as the "man for others" in the Spirit which not only transforms His own human reality and experience, but explodes the situation and significance of that humanity into the whole human situation and human history, we can see that to be "in Christ," to be "in the one Spirit" is not just something which happens for our own sakes. It is meant to make us, like Jesus, "men for others" in that same Spirit, expanding the meaningfulness of our very own human existence and experience beyond the limits of our own history and experience to the whole of human existence and experience. The experience of "church," then, should not be the experience of entering the safe harbor, the place of privilege; it should be the experience of wonder, challenge in our own lives and mission to the lives of others. The question for the Christian is not "What do I get out of it?" It is, rather: "What can I give from it?" and "To whom am I sent?"

Thus, the "gathering" of the church, the *ekklesia,* is at once the experience of the transformation of one's life in a new vision, experience and pattern of action, but it is, at the same time, an experience of one's value and meaning for others, for other humans, for any human. Once again, this is an aspect of the Christian experience which has a relatively low visibility in the majority of Christian communities. And its low visibility is responsible for the challenge to the significance, the relevance of Christianity. The mere claiming of the many Biblical titles and images of the church from the New Testament, body of the Christ, bride of the Christ, etc., does nothing to enhance the credibility or meaningfulness of the Christian message unless it is also animated by the other side of this experience, the experience of challenge and mission. We use these images so facilely so often, as if it were some achievement of ours, when, if we only reflected honestly we would have to admit that if we were born in a rice paddy in Viet Nam or China, we would in all probability be just as Buddhist or Maoist as anyone else there. It cannot be emphasized too strongly that the experience in which the church is gathered together is an experience of transformation *and* of mission. And it is this experience of transformation *and* mission which grounds experientially what we mean when we speak of the church as *sacrament.* We can talk all we want about divine institution, signs of grace and so on, but all this talk is merely talk, and talk without meaningfulness unless our lives really are signs to and for others, laden with the inner truth of our own experience of the Christian calling. And, as we have noted again and again, this is a matter of spirit, of vision, experience and action—to others and for others out of the transformation within ourselves.

This is another effect of this reflection which has to do with the attitude of Christians toward themselves and the rest of the religious world. We have already alluded to it with the remark that, if we were honest with ourselves, we would admit that if we were born in another part of the world and in another culture, a culture in which Christianity were not such a pervasive

aspect of the prevailing culture, we would in all probability be
Buddhist, Moslem, Jewish, or a member of any of the in-
digenous religions in other parts of the world. For those who
think of Christianity as the safe haven of orthodoxy and salvation this might seem unthinkable. But odds are that it is true
for the vast majority of those of us who call ourselves Christian.
We can talk all we want about the divine grace of the Christian
vocation as if this were a gift straight from God, but this gift
comes to us through human experience, family experience,
cultural experience and so on. And this consideration relativizes
much of the traditional way of thinking of Christianity. It used
to be that you were Christian or not and the matter of being a
Christian was a matter of baptism and visible membership in a
visible Christian community. But, given the growing knowledge
and familiarity with non-Christian religion and the careful study
of the human valence of our religious symbol system, we can
no longer look at our own experience, indeed, our religious
experience of transformation in the Spirit as something unique
in the world. Vatican II alludes to this in its statements of
esteem for the religious experience of non-Christian religious
systems and it insists that the Holy Spirit offers to everyone
the same possibility of association with the paschal mystery
which is usually restricted in our thinking to professed Christians (*Church in the Modern World,* n. 22). Thus, the experience of Christianity no longer has any right to face the religious
experience of the rest of humanity with the attitude that we are
in and they are out, that we are all right and they are all
wrong. To the extent that our religious experience really is
religious experience, we bear a common tradition, a common
quest for the depth of the human in which the reality of the
one God is revealed to us all. This has significant implications
for the way we approach our own Christian life as a sacramental reality. The Christian community is a sign, indeed a
sign which speaks to men of the God who dwells at the depths
of all our experience. And being a sign does not mean that we
seek to share our experience, our Spirit in a language which is

foreign to anyone who does not live in the Christian tradition. Rather It means that we speak in a language which everyone who seeks to be human can know and understand, the language of man, man's condition, man's striving, man's hopes. For it is that language that our profession that Jesus is alive, that Jesus is the Lord has meaning in and for human experience. And that language is not simply a language of words; it is far more a language of deeds, the deeds of love, joy, peace, patience—the language which the Spirit of God, the Spirit of Jesus speaks to the world through the fruits that Spirit bears in the human quality of our lives. Only in this way can our profession of faith have meaning and credibility, for ourselves, for anyone else.

All of this has something important to say for our understanding of the sacramental reality of the Church. In its defense of the liturgical, pastoral and doctrinal tradition of the church, the council of Trent emphasized the fact that that tradition was not just one long history of corruption and venality. And it did so in the language which it had at hand, the language of divine institution. Thus, the life and structures of the church are justified by appeal to the divine law—the number and shape of sacramental signs, the laws about marriage, etc. And whatever is not demonstrably of divine institution, is reductively so because of the divine right of the church to regulate its life and practice. At first sight this might seem today to be quite a pretension. But recent historical studies have shown that this means very much the same thing as our own reflections on the action of God and Jesus in man's history. It is more a defense of the reasonableness and legitimacy of the tradition of church life. That council was very much aware of the corruption and venality of which the church was accused and tried, more or less successfully, to reform them. The point here is what happened to those conciliar statements as they passed into the hands of later theologians and theological handbooks. What emerged was an emphasis on the fact that a sacrament has the power to "confer grace" because it is an

action instituted by Christ to give grace, with the promise that
grace would be conferred if the sign was properly performed
by a legitimate minister. Thus the basic principle of the power
of a sacramental action was the principle of validity, a principle
usually based in turn on the principle of apostolic succession, a
succession in which the power to validly perform sacramental
signs has been legitimately handed down through the centuries
in an unbroken line.

But from the perspective of these reflections, we can begin
to see a deeper meaning for validity than mere legal justification
cum divine guarantee from the beginning. The validity which
we seek is a human validity, a meaningful validity within the
context of human experience. It is the power which a sign has
to confer its meaning meaningfully and effectively to human
experience in such a way that one knows that the reality brought
to expression is true, true to human existence and true for
human existence. In this perspective we need not simply reject the older framework for understanding because in that
framework as in ours the power of sacramental reality to convey the reality it brings to expression resides in the reality of
spirit, the Spirit. Thus, it is not a matter of the transmission of
a magical kind of power which is in question. Rather it is the
matter of the transmission of a spirit, the Spirit of Jesus, the
Spirit of God. The validity of the Christian community as a
sign of the grace of human existence as this is revealed in the
resurrection of Jesus, a sign of the newness of humanity, is
rooted in the human experience which mediates the vision of
the living Lord Jesus. It is, then, a matter of spirit, a matter of
truth.

Thus, the validity of the church as sacrament, the power
which the church has to embody and convey the meaning of
the resurrection of Jesus, is a matter of the *truth of the church*.
And the truth in question here is not merely a matter of logical
coherence or demonstration. It is a matter of an *experienced*
truth within the framework of human existence. It is not abstract, but concrete; the meaningfulness of the sacramental

church resonates with the very structures of human existence and finds it power there in that resonance. This kind of truth convinces without argument, before logic. It shines out of the lives of those who are true. It conveys the living meaning for human life of the fact that Jesus is risen from the dead, with all the transformation of human vision and human hope which this meaning is, and in this way conveys God's own truth into the lives of those who can receive this truth in the newness of the new Spirit. For God's truth is not a series of propositions, statements. Rather, it is God's very reality and that reality for us is the unfailing faithfulness of God to His promise, which is that He will always "be there." In our lives, this means that our own existence, our own history is unfailingly grounded in goodness, value, meaningfulness. Human existence is infallibly worthwhile, absolutely possible.

But God's truth, a faithfulness to His promise which is definitively revealed as the resurrection of Jesus enters and transforms human history and experience, is without meaning, without power, unless it brings about a deep human truth. For it is in our truth that God's truth enters our history and exerts its transforming and liberating power. It is that absolute fidelity which makes us free, free to be human in a new and deeper way. Thus it is a question of the church as the sacrament of God's truth, absolutely grounding the value of human existence. But that truth depends for its historical power for the human on *our* truth, our truth to the meaning of the resurrection of Jesus within our lives, our experience. The basic truth of the church is the answer to the question, "Are all, in actual fact, baptized into one body in the one Spirit?" Has the resurrection-pentecost event really taken place in our own lives? What is the character and quality of our vision, our experience, our action? Are they truly freed for the human? Are they in fact hope-filled and hope-sharing? If this is in fact so, then we are true to the risen Lord Jesus, to God in their one Spirit. And, if this is in fact so, we are a power-laden sign to the world and for the world of God's own truth. If this is not in fact the case, then we are truly powerless, an ineffective, empty sign, a token gesture which can only convey cynicism and despair for the human itself. The power of the church as sacrament is in its truth, the truth of our lives—and this is all a matter of spirit, the Spirit.

It is this Spirit and this truth which become visible in the experience of being the Church of the Christ. And it is important to keep in mind that this Spirit and truth are not gifts which are given once and for all in the experience in which the meaning of the resurrection of Jesus enters our lives and history. It is true that this Spirit overtakes our vision, experience and action in the transformation which takes place out of which we can say that Jesus is the Lord, our Lord. But this Spirit is still a pledge, a gift which enters our lives and becomes there a value that must constantly be realized in the midst of the ambiguity which forms so much of the pattern of human existence. This Spirit and truth are values which must constantly be gained over and over again in the on-going moments of our time. They are vocations for the church of the Christ, not its definitive realities achieved once and for all at the beginning of its or our history.

However, we know that there are many spirits and many truths. And, consequently, our reflections must center on the characteristics which distinguish the experience of the Spirit of the Christ and the church of the Christ. A long tradition gives us four distinctive characteristics for the church of the Christ, and we must turn our attention to the meaning of these characteristics within our human experience. For these characteristics tell us what kind of people we should be, if we are to be the powerful and, more important, the credible sign of the resurrection to and for the people whose lives our lives touch.

The Call to Unity

The first and most important characteristic of the Spirit which forms the background for the vision, experience and action of the church of the Christ is that it draws men into *unity*. We find a strong emphasis on this in the experience of those who first witnessed to the resurrection. It forms a great part of the exhortation which Paul wrote to the Christians of Corinth. In the midst of the bickering over who was the best apostle, parties arose among the Corinthians. Paul deplored this division and excoriated the competing schools of thought, this because of the factions into which it divided a community which was supposed to be uniquely one. And accordingly he encourages them to be truly one in spirit, of one mind and judgment (1 Cor 1:10–30). Their lack of unity was a judgment which condemned their Eucharist in the shape of the sick, the weak, even the dead (11:27–32). Even the charismatic gifts which arose out of the Spirit of the Christ in the community have one purpose: the common good of all (12:4–11). And all these gifts arise out of one fact: the one Spirit in which all have been baptized into the one Body (12:12–13). But his exhortation reaches its peak when he comes to the heart of what this unity should be. It consists in the *love* which the members of the community should have for one another. It is the patience, the understanding, the fidelity of that love which shows that this is the Spirit of the Christ which animates the life of the community (13:4–7). It is this love which abolishes every kind of division and distinction, so that there are no longer Jews and Greeks, no longer slaves and freemen, not even male and female (Gal 3:27)—all are one. But this unity is a unity in the experience of love, a love which shows itself in lowliness, meekness, patience, forebearance and the eagerness to maintain this unity of the one Spirit in the bond of peace. And the reality of this love reveals to all the oneness of the Body, the oneness of the Spirit, the oneness of the hope, the one Lord, the one faith, the one baptism, the oneness of the one God who is above all, communicated by all and in all (Eph 4:1–6). And John, looking back on the life of Jesus from the context of his experience of the Spirit sees this as the great central reality of the life of Jesus and His final gift to the world: that His own might be one as He and His Father are one, God in Jesus, Jesus in the Christian, Christians in one another in a unity which proclaims to the world that God has sent Jesus, that Jesus is the Son and that God loves us just as He loves Jesus (Jn 17:20–23). And the closing memory of Jesus finds its formulation in a final command, a new commandment, that we love one another as He loved us, laying down His life for us, that we might have a more abundant life (15:12–17).

Thus, the unity which the Spirit of the Christ achieves in us and calls us to achieve constantly in that Spirit is the unity which is brought about by the fact that we love one another as Jesus loved us. That is a love without condition, without limit. It is a love which is not based on the fact that we are alike or that we do things which always please one another. It is a love which pours our lives out in service of the lives of others, that those lives might be more abundant. And this "pouring out" of our life in the service of others is a love which prizes another person precisely in his otherness. There is a self-serving kind of affection which seeks to project our own needs and desires into the lives of others and to "love" them to the extent that they fulfill our expectations of them. This is not the love of God, the love of Jesus. For the love of God is a love which places us in existence as *ourselves,* in our deepest subjectivity, as completely "other" from God. And this is made manifest in the love which Jesus has for us. This is a love which does not look to merit, to good deeds. As Paul tells us, "It is difficult to imagine anyone dying for a righteous man, although maybe someone might go so far as to die for a good man. But God shows His love for us in that while we were still sinners, Christ died for us." (Rom 5:7–8) It is this absolutely faithful, patient and undemanding love which is the image of that love which contains the experience of the oneness of the community which is one in the Spirit of the Christ.

It is this kind of love which liberates in each person the capacity to be most truly himself and is, at the same time, that which makes us who love in this way most truly ourselves. It is a love which speaks to the otherness of the other person and affirms that very otherness, saying, in effect, that for you to be you (not some projection of myself) is the best thing in the world. This is the kind of love which seeks to evoke the very subjectivity of the other, seeks to speak to a person's deepest interior. We can see that this is truly a creative love, a love which brings a person into being and operation *as himself*. And we can see how it is that this quality of vision and action can bring about the most fundamentally necessary human experience, the deep knowledge and faith that what God said in the creation of man is true, "He saw that it was very good" (Gen 1:31). For this is, in the last analysis, the most crucial act of faith which any of us must make, the act of faith in the goodness, the value, the worthwhileness of our own life and history. And this is the purpose of this experience of the unique unity which is brought about by the Spirit of the Christ.

It is from this base, then, that we can see that the unity of the Church of the Christ is a far cry from the political or social uniformity which has passed for Christian unity. The unity of the church is meant to deepen and strengthen each and every personal center of existence and to call it to be most itself. It is this conviction which lies behind Paul's insistence that there are many members in the one body, many ways of serving, many individual and personal gifts, many kinds of personal power, but one Spirit, one Lord, one God bringing all these services and gifts into unity (1 Cor 12). The unity within this wonderful diversity is the unity of love (c. 13) which prizes and deepens the individuality of each person in patient and faithful love. The one Spirit of the one God deepens the human in all of us or it is not the Spirit of God.

This kind of unity in love, then, is the vehicle which transforms our spirit and opens up a whole new horizon and background for our own personal existence. There is no program, no plan for this kind of love, only the program of the deep liberation of the human within each person. One can easily see why this profound and deep meaning of the resurrection would be a scandal to the one who lives by external criteria and foolishness for those who think that man is saved by abstract systems of thought. For, in this love, there is a foolishness that is wiser than any wisdom, a weakness which is stronger than any strength. For it is out of this experience of love, with all its power to transform our consciousness in the liberation of the deepest and richest hope, that we can enter most fruitfully into the process of being ourselves, being ourselves in the paradoxical process of giving ourselves in love. And it is out of this love that the creative word of God touches the depths of our lives, "Thou shalt be—be yourself in all the richness of promise that you are!"

It is in this very concrete and human sense, then, that we can speak of the church as sacrament, a sacrament-sign of God's love of us in Jesus, but a sacrament whose reality as sign is embodied in the depth and breadth of the human itself. No secret language here, but a language which speaks immediately and powerfully to the human as such, addressing its depths with a truly creative word. And it is to this unity in love that we must be true if the reality of the church is to have any meaning or power in human history. Otherwise we only have another ideology to give, whose ideas will soon tire and lose their life altogether. It is, once again, all a matter of spirit and truth, the spirit and truth of God's love for us in Jesus, the Christ, reaching into our vision, experience and action to transform, to create the very possibility of being, finally, really human. But, as we have noted, this is a unity which must be won constantly through the faithfulness, the truth of our love for one another. It is a value which must constantly be realized within the pattern and history of human experience. It is a vocation—to constantly become one in the Spirit of Jesus. And this is true not only because this reality only comes into concrete existence historically in the day-to-day pattern of our lives, but also because in order to bring this unity in love into existence we must overcome the incompleteness of our own humanity, the drag which fear, guilt, hatred of ourselves and others exert on our struggle to be human. For it is these dehumanizing facts in our lives which make it impossible to believe who God really is: Love.

The Call to Holiness

The Spirit of Christ is, then, the spirit of oneness—the very oneness of God in Christ and Christ in God but a oneness which comes into concrete historical reality as a unity *for us* in that same Spirit. It brings about a oneness of spirit among us in the reality of our love for one another. And this unity in love is the foundation for the second characteristic of the Spirit of the Christ: holiness. Our concern here is for the experience of holiness. And this immediately could cause us some problems. We are accustomed to think of holy people and holy things as realities which are not for our ordinary human experience. In a sense this could be true. But, if holiness *means* anything, it is something which lies within our human experience—otherwise it is meaningless indeed and useless to talk about it. Until recently, we all have been accustomed to think in terms of Gratian's distinction of the "two kinds of Christians," the real Christian, who offers himself wholly to God, lives a life of celibacy, serves the altar, devotes most of his time to prayer, and the other kind, a second-class Christian, who is allowed to till the soil, give gifts to the church and be married. Holiness was something for the monks and nuns who removed themselves as thoroughly as possible from the human condition to be professionally "holy." But this is a departure from the original experience of Christianity. In Paul's vision, the Spirit which reveals the risen Jesus is a Spirit which at once makes those who have this vision and make this profession holy. It is the Spirit of holiness who establishes Jesus as Son of God in power in His resurrection (Rom 1:4). And it is this same Spirit who takes over the vision of the Christian, making the Christian holy, "You were made holy and just in the name of

the Lord Jesus, the Christ and in the Spirit of our God" (I Cor
6:11). And in this Spirit we experience our election to be God's
holy people, the "saints" (I Cor: 1:2, 24; Rom 1:7; Phil 1:1,
etc.). And this holiness is the holiness of God Himself, which
becomes, in the Spirit of God, our call to be holy as He is (I
Pet 1:15 f.). Paul simply refers to the Christians as "the holy
ones," "the saints." The point is simple, if startling. The experience of being Christian, of being the church, is an experience of holiness.

But our concern here is for the meaning of that holiness in
our own lives, for the meaning of holiness within genuinely
human experience. And when we look at what this holiness has
meant to those who experienced it, we find that it expressed an
"otherness," a distance, difference from "the world." Hence
the historical spectacle of people removing themselves from the
world of men, which is seen as filled with sin and unholiness.
As good and as profitable as this may have been and may still
be, it does not answer our question of meaning, the meaning
of God, the meaning of Jesus, the Christ. For, if God means
God and Jesus means Jesus for everyone, this holiness cannot
be so esoteric and alien to the human condition that the two,
humanity and holiness, are in the last analysis incompatible.

What, then, does holiness mean? When we speak of the
holy, we mean something or someone who belongs to God and
shares in the sacredness of God. It is something which is set
apart from the world and sanctified in that it belongs somehow
to God. And it is holy because it shares in the "otherness" of
God. The primitive attitude toward the holy, then, shared in
the terror (reverence) which man has in the face of that which
is totally different from his ordinary experience of himself and
his world. And so he surrounds the holy with a series of taboos
which protect not so much the holy as man himself, for the
penalty for injured majesty is death. We find this attitude
clearly enough in the Old Testament. Man either walks bare-
foot or not at all on the "holy ground" where God comes to
earth. When man's conduct draws God out of heaven, His

coming is a terrible thing indeed, accompanied by thunder, lightning, darkness, etc., and men tremble with fear. And we feel something of this in the appearances of the risen Jesus, the fear which greets the risen Jesus (Mk 16:8; Lk 24:37; etc.). There is meaning to this fear, as we shall see, but it is important to get behind this mythology to find the meaning of this holiness in the context of the human.

Getting behind the representations of the "otherness" of God in terms of our own human experience, we can see something which recalls our reflection on the life of spirit. In that reflection we found that spirit has its own "otherness" from the world, from everything which seeks to engulf and devour the life of spirit. What seeks to engulf and devour spirit is precisely that which we can call "the world." It is the dead hope which comes from seeing ourselves as simply continuous with the predictable and ineluctable forces of "nature." For the primary experience of spirit is precisely the experience of discontinuity, the experience of being "other" from the relentless movement of natural forces. As spirit, we are confronted with our own concrete existence, with all that we are at this moment, all that we have become, for better or for worse. And this confrontation is a practical confrontation, a confrontation with the question of our own lives, our own history. What will we be? What will we do about our own very concrete and individual human existence? We are not ruled dumbly by the winds and waves; our existence, our history, is our own, if indeed we are spirit. In this very deep human sense, then, we are set apart from the world *in our very humanity*. To be truly human is an event of liberation, liberation from the relentless patterns of movement which the "world" is. And this does not only refer to the process of dumb nature. We can and do become one with that process to the extent that we reject the specifically human and settle into the patterns of day-to-day life which swallow up real consciousness, which make the days march by one after another, one like the other, without growth, without achieving more than a salary, a little status, the trap-

pings of "well-being" devoid of any answer to the summons
for more being which spirit, in fact, is. To be one with the
"world" in this sense is a neglect or a positive refusal *of our
own humanity.* Here we stand, we can do no other. God help
us. Amen. God help us, indeed!

From this reflection, we can see that we are meant to be
holy indeed. Our consciousness is holy in its call to break
away from the patterns of being at home in this world, to enter
into the process of becoming a living spirit, not driven by brute
forces or human forces, but being truly "other" from them in
the entrance into the true process of our own humanity. Our
time is sacred, because it is the place of our liberation from
"the world" in our concrete power of decision; it is the place
of our being "other" from the dead chronologies of the ineluctable and predictable and of our entrance into the experience of truly being the "free-born," *liberi.* Our freedom is a
truly holy place, for it is the event in which we actually experience our liberation from dead and ineluctable force and our
liberation to be truly spirit, to live in spirit and in truth. And
our hope is sacred, holy in that it is the realism of this hope
which sustains our very "otherness" from "this world." For it
is that hope which gives meaning and value to our own very
particular lives. It is that hope which gives us the vision that
sees spirit as worthwhile, as possible, in spite of every force
which seeks to deny it. Our holiness is the holiness of being
holy spirit, for spirit is holy, different from the "world," liberating from the "world." Spirit, our experience of our own
consciousness, time, liberation and hope, is the *holy* place, the
place where the reality of God enters human history and reveals itself bit by bit in the fabric of our own very particular
history.

And we are not all that different from "primitive man," for
we, too tremble before the holy, fear it, reverence it. For we
are not only spirit, we are also "flesh," one with "the world" in
our hankering after security, ease, well-being. Thus the challenge which spirit is within us is a challenge which we fear. And

our fear is precisely the fear of really being and becoming spirit, more being. For in order to become more, we must have the courage to leave behind what we are, what we have. To gain all, we must be willing to lose all. And in this, we fear transcendence, the transcendent in our own lives. The sun goes dark indeed, as we lose the light of the familiar and comfortable surroundings of well-being and open ourselves to the "more" of spirit. The stars of our mundane hopes, status, more money, more power, more sex, fall from the sky as the challenging invitation to transcendence confronts us. Here is a theophany indeed, and out of our comfort and well-being, we tremble in fear before it. And in our own subtle ways, we create our taboos. For it looks for all the world as if we will die if we dare enter into that place. But this death is a different kind of death. It is a death to going values, to status, to the dog-eat-dog values of the world of well-being.

From this we can see what a deep conversion, what a deep repentance, is required of us if we are to enter into the very processes of the human, into the holy. For the answer to the invitation to transcendence which the human spirit is demands that we turn our back on the trappings of well-being and change our whole mind-set (*meta-noia*), go beyond the values of well-being to those of real being—more being. What this means in each man's life is up to each man to find. But it always means becoming more human, and more holy precisely in becoming more human. Holiness is indeed the reality of being "other" from "the world," but it is by no means "other" from the human. Indeed, the holy is the human in all its depth and challenge. It is here that holiness takes on a meaning for human existence.

And it is precisely this kind of holiness which is liberated by the event of the resurrection of Jesus and the coming of the *Holy Spirit* into our lives. For it is this event which brings about the "new creation." The important thing is no longer being Jew or Greek, free or slave, not even male or female; in this event everything is made new. But this newness invades the human precisely through the transformation of our vision and experience by the liberation of a radically new hope: the hope made realistic in this transformation and liberation that we can after all be human and not simply play cultural, professional or even personal roles. Through this event, we experience the call to love, the summit of human existence, peace and joy, the blessings of love, faithfulness, gentleness, patience and mildness, the day-to-day shape of love. And it is in this love that our vision, our consciousness, our time, our hopes are transformed. We are indeed a new creation, but in and through our own human experience. Anything else is meaningless for us or pretense.

One final remark on holiness. It might seem that holiness, which is really the transcendent reality of the human itself, since this is a calling to transcend the experience and the limits of the everyday in our lives, looks for a release from that everyday kind of existence. Nothing could be farther from the truth. The reason for this is that, although holiness is a call to transcendence, it is a call for transcendence precisely within the framework of our ordinary existence. What holiness does is not to deliver us from the ordinary facts of human existence, but to transform our very ordinary existence from *within that ordinary existence*. Within the framework of each human vocation, the search and struggle for the human has for its function the deepening of the specifically human in all its forms, in every individual and corporate way there is of being human. Thus, whether one is a laborer, a housewife, a student, a professional man or woman, a politician—a churchman!—one lives each of these vocations in a more and more human way. It is not a matter of an escape to some magic kingdom, but a deeper and more serious entrance into the shape of each of our individual and corporate humanities, in the struggle against the incomplete humanity and the inhumanity that each of us knows dwells in our lives. To be holy is to *be* wholly, in a wholly holy human way.

The Call to Catholicity

This characteristic of the Spirit of the Christ and of the experience of that Spirit in the experience of being the church of the Christ, the experience of holiness, opens up another characteristic of that Spirit. Traditionally, this characteristic has been called *catholicity*. But the long and difficult history of this word can cause problems. Originally, it simply meant the whole church, present in each of its member churches because of Jesus and His Spirit. When the church became an established religion after Constantine, it became a legal title, meaning the correct, the orthodox, the recognized church. And since the reformation, it has become a name for churches which adhere more closely to the ancient forms and uses of Christianity, the Roman Catholic, the Greek Catholic, the Russian Catholic, the English Catholic, etc. The original meaning of the term was one of universality, generality and wholeness. But as the Christian experience defined itself in more and more exclusive terms, the meaning of the term came more and more to be a matter of particularity and exclusiveness. And today, when churches experience more and more unity in their differences, and the human family draws closer and closer together in so many ways, we would be hard pressed to give a concrete meaning to the word. With the growing recognition of the validity of many different religious traditions, one might well raise the question of "catholic" meaning "orthodox," the one and only true way. The divisions between Christian churches and their relative minority among the religions of the world might well raise the question of the truth of "catholic" meaning "universal." And thus, we are forced once again to the question of meaning.

If the catholicity of the experience of being the church of the Christ is not apparent from the institutional forms which have organized this experience over the centuries, we must return to the original experience out of which the confession that Jesus is the Lord, the Christ, arose. And there we find, as we have noted, that that experience was a twofold experience.

It was an experience of an inner transformation of vision which gave a whole new cast to the experience of one's self, one's world and human history. It is the experience of liberation from the divisions, the fears, the hatreds to which human existence and human history seem condemned. Human existence and human history are seen as a new creation, a whole new beginning in the life and fruits which come from the overtaking of our spirit by the Spirit of God, the Spirit of the Christ. For it is this one Spirit who gives us access to the new oneness, oneness with ourselves and oneness with one another, breaking down all the old divisions and calling all men to a unity in love, the perfection, the acme of the human (Eph 2:14 f.). Thus, if the institutional forms of the Christian spirit convey the universal meaning of the resurrection, the Spirit of Christ, the spirit of the Christian certainly are meaningful for the whole of mankind. For this Spirit addresses itself to the human *as human*. Its whole function is the healing of the incompleteness of our own humanity and the liberation of any man to be human in the working and sharing of that Spirit among us. And it is in this Spirit, the holy Spirit, the catholic Spirit that Paul can see and proclaim the one and universal desire of God: that *all men* should be saved and come to the knowledge of the truth (I Tim 2:4). But that truth, as we have noted, is not just a series of propositions; it is rather the reality of experience which propositions formulate and that underlying reality and experience is precisely that of humanity itself. In raising Jesus from the dead and sharing His Spirit with us, God has transformed the human in its actuality and in its possibilities. And it is this experience which drove the first witnesses into the streets to proclaim this new liberation, this new hope to every man. Thus, looking concretely at what the Spirit of God means, we can see that it means the very depth of the human as this is revealed in our relation to the absolute God within our own history and histories and that that Spirit means this through the experience of Jesus as the risen Lord. But all this means that the resurrection of Jesus has its meaning *in the Spirit for the human as such* and thus for all humanity. It is in the pledge which this Spirit is within the structure and content of our concrete human spirit which bears witness to the fact that Jesus, in the way in which He is human now is the first-born of many brethren, so that all creation waits longingly for the revelation of the free-born children of God (Rom 8:18 ff.). Thus the catholicity of the church of the Christ is in the catholicity, the universality of this Spirit, the catholicity of this Spirit as the very meaningfulness of the resurrection of Jesus for all human experience, for all men.

However, the catholicity of this Spirit only becomes a historical reality to the extent that it transforms our spirit, our vision, our experience, our lives and opens us to the human, to all the human. This means that although our love, patience, goodness and so on are directed toward those with whom our lives are shared more immediately, our spirit of unity, holiness and catholicity must be concerned with all the human as human. This means that the spirit of the Christian is a spirit which seeks to deepen the human and eliminate the inhuman in every part of humanity. Perhaps for the first time in history we are able to begin to experience this in a concrete way. The wars of the world are no longer far off from us, but staring us in the face every day, making their claim on our consciences now. The poor and starving of the world may be half the globe away, but their hunger pricks our conscience every day via newspaper, television. Maybe we can only cry out, "This is inhuman and a diminishment of all of our humanity"; maybe we are in a position to make a more positive and direct contribution to the humanity of the masses of the world. But, whatever our position may be, one thing is certain: the spirit of the Christ is a spirit of love and concern for the human as such and thus for the whole of the human situation. It is a catholic Spirit.

The catholicity of the spirit of the Christ is a translation into human vision, experience and action of the very fact that Jesus is *the* Lord, Lord for all men of all time. And the vehicle of this translation is the actual scope of our love and concern for the human as such. If that scope includes only those like ourselves, the white, the black, the rich, the poor, the "in" or the "out," we are actually impeding and diminishing the very Lordship of Jesus, God's very being God. And from this, it is clear that this characteristic of the Christian spirit and experience is not a characteristic which is automatically given to the Christian at the outset of the Christian vocation and experience. It is a value which must constantly come into realization through our human effort; it is a value of the Christian vocation which is at once given as a vocation and constantly to-be-realized. Once again, there is no magic, only the spirit and truth of our own Christian calling which either brings these values and characteristics into historical actuality or does not. To the extent that we are true to the calling of the Spirit of the Christ, these characteristics will be realized, to the extent that we are untrue to that calling, they are not. It is all a matter of Spirit and of truth.

The Call to Apostolicity

The fourth and final characteristic of the Christian spirit and its vision, experience and action is its *apostolicity*. Like the quality of catholicity, this has been used in a substantial and exclusive sense to separate one church from the schismatic and heretical churches. It has meant that the church of the Christ is that community of faith and practice which traces that faith and practice back to the first apostles. But, once again, there are problems here. Very little of the doctrine or order of any church traces back directly to the apostles. The Christian experience has taken place in history and has adapted itself to that broad human history and, in some cases, adapted that history to itself. The present constitution of church order traces back to the late middle ages. Much of the formulation of doctrine is of about the same provenance. But there is an even deeper problem today, the problem of meaning. What does it mean today, within the framework of human experience, to say that the church of the Christ is "built up on the foundation of the apostles and prophets, the Christ, Jesus, Himself being the cornerstone" (Eph 2:20)?

As we have seen in our reflection on the Christ, the meaning of this apostolic character of the Christian spirit and Christian experience is the problem which has faced generation after generation of Christians. The problem has been phrased in the question of whether the Jesus whom we experience as Lord and Christ is the *same* Jesus to whom the first witnesses to the resurrection bore testimony, the *same* Jesus they preached as risen from the dead for us. And, as we have noted there, this is a matter of spirit and truth, of truthfulness to the Spirit of the Christ, to the vision, the experience and the action that that Spirit reveals and to which that Spirit summons us. It is not so much a matter of the same words, the same order, the same liturgy—these can change and, as anyone who has taken the trouble to study the history of church order, doctrine or liturgy can easily see, they have changed and must continue to change if they are to have any continuous meaning to the men for whom Jesus was raised from the dead. And thus if the Spirit of the Christ is the very meaningfulness of the resurrection and all that this has to say to us about the reality of God and of our own lives, the orthodox church is the church which is faithful, true to the Spirit of the Christ in every age, in every culture, in every human experience. Jesus, the Christ is the same yesterday, today and forever in the one Spirit which is His very "divinity," His oneness with God and at the same time, His oneness with us. Jesus is the same Christ in the same Spirit.

As we have also noted the vision and experience which is the fruit of that one Spirit is the twofold reality of transformation and mission. It is a deep transformation of our human vision, experience and action, of our spirit, and it is all this in a deeply human way, which opens up to the struggle and search for the human in ourselves and in every human context. Transformation and mission: transformation of the human and mission to the actuality and the possibility of the human. And in this mission, we are apostolic in the same sense and terms in which the first witness to the resurrection were apostles —sent to bear witness to the meaning of this fact to all men, but that mission arises then and now in the same way, in the same Spirit transforming and commissioning our spirit in the same way, in the liberation of our consciousness, our temporality, our freedom and our hope to be truly spirit, truly human, all of us. Here is the experiential heart of the apostolic spirit. It is not a matter of doctrinal or ethical orthodoxies or ideologies. It is first and foremost a matter of experience, the experience of the Spirit within the structure of our Spirit.

Of course, this understanding of the meaning of apostolicity will find little sympathy or even hearing in the bureaucratic mind and ear. As Karl Mannheim points out, that kind of mind equates the particular order of a particular social structure with order in general and seeks to reinforce its order with philosophies of government which stress the intrinsic necessity of its very human and relative structures and practices. And, because of its emotional and intellectual investment in the going structure and order, it can only see the emergence of new experience, new vision, new patterns of action as dis-order and lawlessness. Thus, rather than entering seriously into the politics of the situation in the search for what is humanly possible in the new situation, the new spirit, it can only react with peremptory decrees, hoping to stem the tide of the new experience. The thought that the human spirit and its historical experience are open-ended realities is unthinkable, and so it seeks to invest its own structures with an eternity of either reason or faith which makes any change a rebellion against some kind of God-given order. But the student of history, be he professional or amateur, knows that orders come and orders go. And, strangely enough, only bureaucrats remain. As has been pointed out, eighty percent of them eventually move from the old order to the new and end up pretty much in the same kind of positions—which shows that their talents are necessary for some sort of social

structure. But the human experience has and will continue to
organize itself in different orders. What remains constant in all
of this? *The human spirit itself!* This is the object of our orders,
our structures—to assist the human spirit in its historical development. And an order or structure which seeks to block the
movement of that wind, to damp that fire attacks the human
spirit in its most important aspect, the aspect of its constant
cry for *more being,* for new being. And it is precisely here, in
the spirit as a cry for more, for the new that the reality of the
risen Jesus speaks to the human spirit in the newness of life
and hope which the Spirit of the risen Jesus is.

Thus, the apostolic spirit is not the spirit of the frozen
forms of a given structure. It is an identity of mission in the
one Spirit. And to be faithful for its own apostolicity, the
church must constantly serve and share this new Spirit, opening up to every human being the wealth of meaning for the
human which the risen Jesus is in His Spirit. And thus, this
apostolicity is not a frozen historical fact, a sort of relay race
in which the baton is passed from generation to generation in
the form of verbal, ethical or structural orthodoxies. Rather
apostolicity is a fidelity to the one Spirit as this Spirit speaks
within the constant changes of human society and culture. But
this fidelity is a fidelity to the meaning of the event of the
resurrection within the context of our moving history. It is
the same Spirit, the same mission, received through the same
experience. The apostolic church is the church which lives out
of and shares this experience, following the Spirit as the Spirit
creates this experience in every age of the church's life. It is a
church searching through history to find who we will be, who
the Christ, Jesus will be, who God will be for us. All this in
the unity and identity of the same Spirit.

Now perhaps we can begin to appreciate in some concrete
way what it means to be and still constantly become the church
of the Christ. It means fundamentally that the event of the
resurrection and pentecost is taking place in the pattern of our
human lives, our human experience. And this is experiential

fact, not just in word or theory. The church of the Christ is the creature of Spirit and Truth, the Spirit who liberates within us the possibilities and capacities of the human and the Truth whom we know as the Son because this resurrection event shows us the true face of a living God, His Father and ours. It is a matter of our spirit and our truth, too, of our truth to the reality of spirit in our lives, of our truth to humanity, ours and every man's.

Further, it is in the context of these reflections on the character and meaning of the experience of being the church of the Christ that we can see what the sacramental reality of church means. It means that the community of belief is a sign to and for all men precisely in terms of their human experience and their human hopes. But the reality of being and becoming the church of the Christ is only a sign to the extent that its members live out of a very particular and concrete spirit, out of a very definite quality of vision and experience and action. We have reflected on the particularity of that Spirit, its oneness in love, its holiness in humanity, its catholicity in its meaningfulness for the human as such, its apostolicity in its fidelity to the Spirit which is the revelation and meaning of the resurrection in and to human existence itself. And we can see how this Spirit has the power to liberate and transform the human. It is only in this sense that we can speak meaningfully of the church as a sign of God, a sign of Christ, with all the power for the deepening and strengthening of the human that this implies. It is only in this sense and this context that we can speak meaningfully of the church as a sign of "salvation," of "grace," for "salvation" is precisely the salvation of the human and the reality of "grace" is the gift of freedom, the freedom to be fully human brought about when the Spirit of the Christ overtakes our spirit. Thus, the power of the church to be the sign of God, the sign of Jesus, the Christ with all this means for human existence lies in the truth of the community of the church. And this truth is not an abstract truth sanctioned by abstract logical demonstrations. It is, rather, a living truth, the truth of the presence of the Spirit of the Christ functioning in a living way in the lives of Christians. It is a truth shared with the world to the extent that that Spirit is shared with every human being who comes into the compass of our lives. It is a truth which is our own fidelity, our own truth to that Spirit, our fidelity, our truth to the human as such. No magic here, only Spirit and truth as living and functioning principles of our lives, our vision, our experience, our action in and to our world. The only power that the church has is the power of Spirit, the power of truth.

It is against this background, then, that we can approach some concrete understanding of what we mean by "sacrament." We have been accustomed to think of sacraments in a relatively automatic way as clear signs which contain a clear reality (grace) which is given to the recipient of the sacrament in the proper performance of the ritual action. The purpose of receiving the sacraments is to "get grace," which we have thought of in rather substantial terms as something which God gives to one who receives the sacrament. And, in the framework of the categories of substantial thinking, the sign is either wrongly done, the sacramental sign is there or it is not, the grace is either given or not given. But once we raise the question of meaning the clear-cut categories of our thinking tend to become fuzzy, less clearly defined. We can continue to say that God is God, Jesus is Jesus, church is church, but these affirmations have little or no meaning in and of themselves. The question of meaning, what these realities mean in terms of our human experience, demands of us that we come to some understanding of what God is *for us,* what Jesus is *for us,* what church is *for us.* God remains God for Himself, and so on, but that aspect of the reality of God which is for Himself is none of our business; it is God's affair to be God for Himself, Jesus' affair to be Jesus for Himself. In this sense, God is God and that is that. But our concern for meaning looks to the relative reality of God, what He is for us. And this means how the reality of God functions within the horizons of our experience. And, as we have seen, this means that God can be more and less God for us to the extent that God has more or less meaning in our lives. Jesus can be more and less the Christ, the Lord, to the extent that His Spirit permeates our spirit. Church is more and less church to the extent that we answer the summons of the Spirit to oneness, holiness, catholicity, apostolicity. This is a more relative and functional view of the reality of God, Jesus, church, but it is the element of our understanding of the reality of God which is most crucial for us for in this framework the realities of God, Jesus and church address the depths and the very solidity of our own human existence and take on *meaning* there.

This context gives a particular cast to what we mean when we speak of the reality of "grace." The objectified and objectifying understanding of grace treats grace as a somewhat fixed reality, indeed, in much of the popular imagination, preaching and teaching, it is in fact quantified. Good actions gain some grace, better actions gain more; bad actions lose grace, worse actions lose more. There is some meaning to this, but the problem with this way of thinking and speaking of the reality of grace is the absence in it of the experiential dimension. And so we must ask the question which cuts across every aspect of religion and theology—the question of meaning: what this means in our human experience. And from our reflections on the themes of God, Spirit, Christ and church, we can see that grace means a relationship with the reality of God. It is a relationship which takes on its concrete reality in the pattern of our own very concrete human experience as we discover the actual meaning of God for us in the history which is our life. And, if we are honest with ourselves, we know that the reality of grace is very much a more-and-less thing. For our relationship with the absolute ground of our human existence is not at all absolute. It takes place within the pattern of our own human growth and transcendence, but that pattern knows a great deal of variation between hope and fear, between courage and commitment to humanity and despair and withdrawal from the demand which our own humanity makes on us. And, in all this, our relation to God grows stronger and weaker, takes on more and less meaning, more and less function in our day-to-day existence. It is not a fixed reality at all, but a very variable and varying relationship, and this within the varieties of our human experience.

The Church: The Sacrament

The reality of grace which we are considering, then, is the reality of *human existence itself* as this is more or less grounded, more or less liberated, for its own humanity, more or less hopeful, more or less loving. The reality of grace, like everything we have considered this far, is a matter of spirit and truth, and we know that we are very much more and less spirit, more and less true. And it is in this context that we must reflect on the meaning of "sacrament," if we are to speak meaningfully and honestly in terms of our own experience. And it is out of this context that we will address ourselves to the question of the meaning of those sacramental actions which make up the major portion of our experience as practicing Christians.

A sacramental action is, in Augustine's terms, *the sign of a sacred reality,* or, as later theology stated it, a *sign of grace.* St. Thomas Aquinas added to this general definition the element of active sanctification: a sacrament is a sign of a sacred reality which is actually sanctifying someone. By this, St. Thomas means that the sacred reality which is expressed in the sacramental sign is a reality which is actually having its sanctifying effect in one's life. And the way in which the sacred reality brings about its effect is through the profession of faith of a believing community. As the community makes public profession of the sacred reality which is the central value of its existence as a community, this sacred reality is deepened in the spirit of the community; the sacred value becomes more and more a functioning aspect of the community's vision, experience and action. This is a phenomenological definition of sacrament; it describes the practice of any sacramental religion. Our question and reflection, however, is directed toward the specific "sacred reality" which forms the content of our Christian sacramental religion. What is the meaning which is contained in and conveyed by our own sacramental action?

Our reflections to this point have let us see that this meaning is a very concrete and specific one: Jesus. The Christian sacrament contains and conveys the meaning of Jesus for the depth of our humanity. And, in this sense, the content of the Christian sacrament is the Spirit of Jesus, the Christ. For that Spirit is, as we have seen, the very meaningfulness of the risen Jesus for our lives; it is the background which gives the Christian character to our vision, experience and action. And that Spirit is the Spirit of God, the background for the human experience of Jesus, the concrete shape of His "divinity." To the extent that we come to share in that Spirit, to the extent that it takes over our Spirit, becoming the background for our vision and experience, the reality of God enters our life and functions there—through Jesus, the Christ in the Spirit. This is, concretely and specifically, the content of the Christian sacrament. It is in this Spirit that the absolute reality of God enters and functions within the relativity of our human experience. It is in that Spirit that God becomes God for us, that Jesus becomes Lord for us. Thus, the "grace of the sacrament," the sacred reality which comes to expression in the sacrament is the grace of Jesus for us, the Spirit of Jesus, the Lord. This is the concrete shape which the Christian experience gives to the reality of God, the deepest grace within our human experience.

But there is a far more important aspect to this reflection on the meaning of the sacramental life of the church, and that is how this grace comes into being and operation within our experience, what it means there. And this involves some reflection on the function of sign-acts in our experience. A sign-act is the act of self-expression. It is an action in which we attempt to formulate some aspect of our own "interior" personal reality and communicate this to the "outside," to the world around us. In terms of our reflection on the reality and experience of spirit, we can describe the sign-act as "spirit rising to visible form" in our expression of the vision, experience and action which make up the concrete content of our being spirit. And this is not a casual, unnecessary process. It is an essential process of human existence. For the reality of spirit, of our own personal identity is not a fixed, given quantity. It is a *process,* and, indeed, the two-way process of our receiving the reality of the world of people and things around us into our own vision and experience and of our "talking back" to that world out of the vision and experience which we create from the way we integrate what we receive from the world around us. To be human, to be spirit, is a process, indeed a dialogical process in which we are in continual conversation with the world of people and things which is the context for our existence. The absolute refusal or incapacity to enter into this conversation has a name: catatonia, a complete withdrawal from the human. It is also called death. In either case it is the refusal or incapacity to move in a human way, be this physical or emotional or both. Thus, to the extent that human existence is human and functioning, it is a constant symbolic process. Our "inner reality" embodies itself in all sorts of languages, verbal, "body-language," all sorts of sign-acts, and in that very process continually comes into being precisely as human. Freedom is at best an abstract and theoretical reality unless it expresses itself in the decisions and commitments which make up the pattern of our action in and to the world. Spirit is only spirit to the extent that it forms the counter-pole to our bodily reality, to the extent that it is actually functioning as the background or horizon out of which we live and express ourselves in bodiliness in and to the world. This is not a matter of a casual decision to express one's self; one cannot be one's self unless one expresses one's self in and to the world. To be human is to be a symbolic process. Withdrawal from this process is the death of the human in us; the impeding of the process is dehumanizing.

Thus the context for understanding the reality and function of the sign-act is the human process itself. Sign-acts serve to express the reality of our own concrete human existence and, in so doing, they are the very being and operation of our humanity. In the process of mutual self-expression we become ourselves and the world becomes the world for us. And from this we can see that the power of these acts to bring the human into being *depends on their truth,* the truth of our faithfulness to being and becoming spirit in a truly human consciousness, freedom and hope. If we are inhuman, untrue to our own humanity, we can only communicate and share inhumanity to the world around us. But this is drawn a little too clearly. We know in fact that we are not fully human or fully inhuman, only more and less human, more and less inhuman. And this depends on the quality of our actual concrete spirit, the quality of our vision, our experience, our action, this in the quality of our consciousness, our liberation and our hope. Sign-acts are not magic, they cannot produce something which is not there. Their power lies in the faithfulness with which we enter into our own processes of self-transcendence. Apart from this, they cannot function to bring about the human within us or around us. Once again, it is all a matter of spirit and truth. And from this, we can see that our sign-acts serve more and less to bring the human into existence and operation, because beside the depth of our own truth there lives the lie that we also are, a lie which is not a matter of words, but a matter of the very quality of our lives, more and less true.

It is out of this context, then, that we can approach a concrete understanding of the meaning and function of the sacramental life of the church. Sacraments are "signs of grace," sign-acts in which the reality of "grace" comes into being and operation in the life of the Christian and the Christian community, this in those actions in which the Christian and the community speak out in word and action the inner reality of the Spirit which makes us Christian, the Spirit of God and the Christ. And from this point of view we can see that the Christian himself, the concrete individual Christian community itself is the basic sacramental reality in whom God, through Christ and in their Spirit, dwells and operates in and for the world. (Bear in mind, however, that we are speaking positively here and not in an exclusive sense.) It is the very human life of the Christian and the Christian community which is the first flowering of the Spirit of the Christ, the place where that Spirit bears its fruit in and for the world. The Christian and the Christian community are meant to be the "sign of the Spirit," *the* grace in which the reality of God touches and transforms human life. This is the place where the Spirit of God, the Spirit of the Christ, rises to visibility and achieves its effects. This is the place, within the very humanity of the Christian and the Christian community, where God becomes God for us, Christ becomes Lord in actual fact in the Spirit which animates, transforms and liberates our own human vision, experience and action. It is in this concrete sense, then, that we can speak of the church as sign of grace, i.e., in terms of the concrete individual lives which Christians lead. It is only in that sense that any particular aspect of action of the church as a community that the church can be said to be the "sacrament of the Christ" in actual fact.

This has an important implication for our understanding of the power of any specific sacramental action in the life of the church, whether it be the seven cultic sacraments, the preaching or teaching of the church, its works of love and service. And this is the fact that the power of the church as sacrament or any aspect of its life as a "sign of grace" depends on the *truth* of the church, the *truth* of the concrete lives Christians lead as individuals and as a community. And this truth is found in whether or not the Spirit of God, the Spirit of the Christ, is actually gathering the church to God, to Jesus, the Lord. And, concretely, this is a matter of experience, the experience of the

Spirit. It is a matter of the truth of the transformation and liberation of our vision, our experiences, our action in the experience of our own spirit. The basic truth and power of any sacramental act of the church depends for its power on the quality of our consciousness, on the extent of our liberation, on the depth and breadth of our hope. If this transformation and liberation is not being sought and achieved to some extent, then there is simply no power in our sacramental life. It is all empty signs, containing and signifying nothing. And all this means that our primary concern in the practice and theology of sacraments must be a concern for truth—*our own truth,* our truth to the very task of being human as this is liberated and revealed within our own experience by the Spirit of God, the Spirit of the Christ. It is only to the extent that that Spirit blossoms in our concrete lives in the fruits which it brings about in our lives, love, joy, peace, patience, and so on, that our sacramental life really "contains the grace which it signifies," i.e., brings to expression.

We can talk all we want about the *ex opere operato* efficacy of our sacramental life, but this is meaningless unless the absolute and unfailing truth of God is met and received in our own truth. For all *ex opere operato* says to us is that God is true, absolutely true, unfailingly faithful in His love for us. But that love, that truth, have no meaning in human life and experience unless they live and function within our own truth. The *opus operatum* is only half the picture, an essential half, it is true, but a meaningless half without our own *opus,* which is our spirit, our truth. We must, in any of our concerns for our sacramental life, go beyond the signs to the meaning which they should contain and convey, to the Spirit, our own spirit, and judge everything in terms of our own truth, the truth of the lives we lead day by day.

Thus, our concern for the meaningfulness of Christianity shows us where our concern should lie for sacramental life— for our truth to God and His Christ in their Spirit forming and transforming the depths of our spirit. But, as we well know, our lives are not all truth and probably never will be. Our lives are and will continue to be a striving for truth out of the context of truth and falseness which are in us. Truth, our own truth, is something for which we must struggle constantly all our lives. We must be content then, to rejoice in what truth we have gained, and to regretfully acknowledge the falseness, falseness to ourselves, to the reality and life of spirit, of the Spirit which persists within our experience. And this means that our own sacramental reality and sacramental life are never completely true. It always was, is and always will be more or less true, more or less grace-filled, grace-communicating. Paul's images of the church as the spotless unwrinkled bride is as eschatological as they come! We are spotted and wrinkled indeed, but calls to clean up the spots and smooth out the wrinkles in our service of the human wherever it is, wherever we are. Thus, our sacramental life is no place for us to be secure and boastful. It is a place where we are called to serve one another and the world in which we live, making whatever truth the Spirit of God, the Spirit of His Christ, has managed to achieve in our lives visibly available to be shared and communicated with God's world. Once again, there is no magic to it. If we do not bring this truth to realization in our own lives, no one else can do it for us, not even God. And thus our sacramental life and celebration must be a constant question to us, a constant challenge. Are we true or false? If we are true, how true are we? If we are false how false are we, why are we false? As we face these questions, these challenges, with honesty perhaps our sacramental life will take on more truth, more of the reality of spirit, more of the reality of the Spirit. And in and through our lives, God will become more and more our God, Jesus will become more and more our Lord. It's all a matter of spirit and truth.

The New Creation

Against the background of our reflection on God, Spirit, Jesus and Church, we can approach some concrete understanding of the meaning of the particular sacramental actions which form the pattern of the cultic life of the church. Our reflections will be concerned with those sacramental actions which make up the majority of sacramental experience in the day-to-day life of the Christian community: the meaning of Christian initiation, the meaning of the eucharistic celebration and the meaning of forgiveness. And, once again, our concern in these reflections is a concern for *meaning*, a concern for the human experiences which these sacramental actions should contain and promote. From what we have seen up to this point, we can see that this experience is a matter of spirit, of the concrete background for vision, experience and action which forms the horizon against which we live our lives in our world. And, as we have seen in our reflection on the meaning of the resurrection of Jesus, we can see that the Christian spirit is a new spirit, the transformation of our spirit by the Spirit of Jesus, the Spirit of God, as this new capacity for vision and experience overtakes our spirit. And our first reflection has to do with the meaning and content of the Spirit in the context of the sacramental actions which signify and bring about incorporation into the Christian community.

The New Spirit

The experience of Spirit which is the principle of our incorporation into the Christian community can best be described in Paul's description of the character of Christian life: the new creation. This is an expression which brings out the fact that the Christian experience should be an experience of reconciliation and unity between man and God, between man and man. In the second letter to the Corinthians, he uses this idea to ground the courage he has in his commission to preach the gospel. He no longer looks at people from the point of view of stale human expectations, but from the totally new point of view which came with his own inner transformation and commission in his experience of the resurrection of Jesus. "If anyone is in Christ, he is a new creation; the old has passed away, behold, the new has come" (II Cor 5:17). And this whole change in vision and reality is from God, who "was in Christ reconciling the world to Himself" (18-19). And in the context of the arguments about the necessity of circumcision, he insists that the division among Jewish and other Christians is wrong, that circumcision or the lack of it means nothing; what counts is the new creation (Gal 6:15). This reflection on the meaning of the sacraments of Baptism and Confirmation will center on this experience, the experience of being a new creation in the Christ.

The theological and pastoral tradition of part of the western church has reflected on and practiced the sacramentalizing of this mystery in two distinct stages, Baptism and Confirmation. The eastern churches have traditionally celebrated these sacraments in a close unity in which Confirmation is administered in conjunction with Baptism and the first participation in the Eucharist. Latin countries have celebrated Confirmation in a close unity with the first communion. But this reflection will focus on these sacramental actions as a unity under the general theme of the new creation. This does not mean that this is an advocacy for any particular pastoral situation and

practice. When theologians and liturgists gather to consider
what can be done pastorally about confirmation, the theologians
generally end up telling the liturgists that whatever works
pastorally seems to be agreeable theologically both from the
standpoint of precedent and of significance—this on the basis
that sacraments are for people and that whatever has been
done obviously can be done. Thus, while we can see the obvious
distinction between the celebration of Baptism and Confirmation, we will consider them in the deep unity of their significance.

The basis for this unity of experiential meaning should be
apparent from our consideration of the character of the experience of the resurrection. It is out of that experience that the
fundamental Christian confession that Jesus is alive, that He is
the Lord arises. And it is this experience and confession which
characterize the Christian spirit and the Christian life. But, as
we have seen on our reflection on the meaning of the resurrection, this confession arises out of a deeply changed and renewed capacity to see, experience, act—in a word, out of a
transformed and renewed spirit. And the transforming and
renewing principle which makes this confession possible is the
Spirit in which alone the confession that Jesus is the Lord is
made possible. The Easter event in which we are buried with
Jesus and raised in Him to a newness of life (Rom 6:3–11) is
an event which takes place in our experience to the extent that
our spirit is overtaken by *the* Spirit, the Spirit of God, the
Spirit of Jesus, a Spirit which transforms our vision, experience
and action by opening out the radically new possibilities of
human existence in the works and fruits of that Spirit. The
meaning of Jesus is the Spirit of Jesus; the meaning of Easter
is Pentecost. These two are really two inseparable aspects of
one event, the transformation of our life, the renewal of our
power to live from within ourselves in a new spirit. And it is
only in that Spirit that the meaningfulness and the demands of
the resurrection of Jesus make themselves felt within our experience. In Paul's words, "In one Spirit we are all baptized

into one body" (I Cor 12:13). And from the perspective of these reflections, we can see that this means that it is the transformation which is the fruit of the Spirit which makes our incorporation into the body of the Christ a reality.

Thus, we will reflect on the sacraments of Baptism and Confirmation as a unity, the unity of the meaning of the Christ, whose meaning and demands on our life are present in and to our lives in the one Spirit.

Further, the focus of this reflection will be broader than the liturgical action in which the reality of Baptism and Confirmation is symbolically celebrated. Our emphasis here is on the *meaning* of that liturgical action. And this means that we will focus on the experience of Spirit which forms the on-going experiential *truth* of this sacramental reality. It is only out of this clear context that we can have any concrete appreciation of what we are about in the matter of infant Baptism and/or Confirmation where spirit (vision, experience and action) comes to a low visibility indeed. Thus, our reflection will center on what it means to be a "new creation" in terms of a developed human consciousness, vision, experience and action. For it is only in this framework that we can actually discern and appreciate in anyone the living and functioning truth of this baptismal reality. And, what is perhaps more important, it is only in this context that we can discern and appreciate the living and functioning truth of this new creation in our own lives. For the reality of our incorporation into the Christ is not merely the matter of a moment. It is *sacramentum permanens,* an ongoing and permanent reality which rises to expression in the whole fabric of our human existence if it is true in any real way at all. Thus our reflection will center on the meaning of Baptism *if and when* Baptism is a living and functioning truth in a person's life. It is out of this context that we can approach some concrete and experiential understanding of the meaning and implications of the "new creation."

Paul's description of the "new creation" situates this reality in a specifically human context. As we have seen, in his statement to the Corinthians, it is those who are "in Christ" who are the new creation; it is in them that the old has passed away and has become new. And the closing words to the Galatians place this reality in a specifically human religious context as a reality which transcends the old distinction between men brought about in circumcision. For the new creation is something that has been brought about in Jesus' resurrection from the dead and the fulfillment of its meaning in the lives of Christians. For the new creation is accomplished in us by our being created "for good works" in Christ (Eph 2:10). For it is in Jesus, through the mystery of His death and resurrection, that the old distinctions between Jew and Gentile are erased, that those who were far from God are brought near, that the divisions between men are dissolved and what was once a twofold mankind is created into one new man (2:15). Paul treats this new oneness in man like a garment with which we are urged to clothe ourselves as if we were going to a great banquet. He encourages the Ephesians to be renewed in spirit and thus to "put on" the new man who has been created in a new reference to God in righteousness and the holiness which comes out of a new truth (4:23–24). This is a new creation, like the first in the image and likeness of God, but this creation is aimed at a new way of being God's acquaintances, i.e., in Jesus, the Christ. And it is this new humanity which we "put on" when we put off the old (Col 3:10).

The "new creation," then, does not so much change the world around us as it changes us in the world. And this transformation brings about a new "nature" in us. But this "nature" is not an abstract humanity, a different kind of concept of humanity in general. Rather, it is most concrete. It gives new content, new direction to our own concrete historical human existence. Paul characterizes this new content as "righteousness" and the "holiness of truth." And the direction of this newness of human existence is phrased in the Greek word *epignosis* (knowledge); the "new nature" is in the constant process of being renewed by the author of the new nature, this in the direction of knowledge. This sounds just fine, but we must ask what this means for Paul and for ourselves.

The "righteousness" in question might bring to mind a kind of "good reputation with God" which is the fruit of doing the right thing by God. This is certainly part of what Paul means, but the righteousness of which he speaks means far more. For the righteousness (*dikaiosune*) of which Paul speaks is first of all God's own righteousness. In the letter to the Romans, Paul goes to great lengths to show that the righteousness of unswerving faithfulness of God to the promise which He makes in history (c. 3). This is a faithfulness which is not impeded even by our sin. As a matter of fact, it is precisely in our sinfulness that God's faithfulness becomes apparent in the fact that He has set Jesus up as the place of reconciliation and mercy (3:31–36). Thus, rather than being an obstacle to God's faithfulness to His promise, our own infidelity, our own lack of faithfulness, righteousness, serves only to show all the more clearly how unswerving is God's firmness in His faithfulness to be our God. It is a matter of fidelity, unconditioned and unswerving faithfulness in love for us, a love shown most clearly in mercy and forgiveness.

This is the "righteousness" which forms the content of the "new nature" out of which we live and which we fashion as we live in faith-full-ness. It is a righteousness which is not abstract or legalistic. Rather, its face is the face of our own faithfulness to the reality of God, and the promise and challenge which this is in our lives. Paul uses the example of the unswerving commitment of Abraham. There was hardly any promise of life in his withered genitals or in Sarah's barren womb. Yet, in spite of the seeming impossibility of the challenge which the reality of God placed into his life, Abraham lived steadfastly in hope that the promise would be fulfilled and committed himself to God and His promise without deviation, more or less. Thus, the renewing transformation which takes place in the "new creation" is a call to a new faithfulness to God in the faithfulness of our response to the promise which the reality of God reveals within our lives. We are a "new man" in this call and challenge. Further, this new call to an unconditioned faithfulness is a new sanctification, a new holiness. But this new holiness finds its form precisely in *truth,* the truthfulness of our commitment to God in terms of our faith, our being true to the calling which the reality of God reveals in our lives. In this very concrete and historical way, then, we come to share in the righteousness and the holiness of God, a righteousness and holiness which find their historical shape in the reality of our own truthfulness to the meaning and challenge of the God of promise. It is out of the fulfillment of this vocation that the direction of the new creation is realized: the "knowledge of God." And the knowledge in question is not simply an intellectual knowledge of abstract or indifferent facts about God; it is the knowledge of the mysterious One whose concrete identity emerges precisely from a pattern of mutual unconditioned acceptance and faithfulness to one another. It is a deep and total kind of personal knowledge which comes out of a shared history, a knowledge concrete in its actualization in the very specific events of a lived human life.

But this is not all there is to the new creation. It is far more specific. For the new creation comes about to the extent that a person is "in Christ." And from our reflection on the meaning of Jesus, the Christ, we can see that this takes place when the meaning of the resurrection of Jesus becomes functional in a person's life. We are "in Christ" in actual experiential fact when the risen Jesus forms the actual historical center for the processes we call "living." And, as we have seen, this is a matter of spirit, of the Spirit of Jesus overtaking our spirit and forming the context out of which we live. In Paul's words, "In one Spirit we have all been baptized into one body . . . and all of us have drunk of one Spirit" (I Cor 12:13). Paul's point in this statement is pointed toward the fact that in this Spirit all the old divisions between Jew and Gentile have been wiped away; but the important point that we wish to stress is that this is a matter of Spirit, the Spirit of Jesus, the

Spirit of God, functioning within our spirit, forming the experiential background for our own vision, experience and action which makes us to be "in Christ" not simply in name or title, but in actual and concrete experiential fact. It is in this experiential fact that the reality of Baptism is a vital and powerful functioning force in our lives, within our experience. For it is in and out of this Spirit that our own righteousness or faithfulness comes constantly into being as we live out of the meaning of the mystery of Jesus which is His Spirit. It is out of this Spirit that our truth comes constantly into being and operation as it forms background for our consciousness, our experience of and functioning in time, our liberation and our hope. Just as in the first creation the Spirit of God hovered over the primeval chaos and bore the word, the structure and meaning of creation, and the world came into being, so, too, in the new creation, it is that same Spirit, hovering over the meaninglessness and hopelessness of human existence which bears the Word, Jesus the Lord, which forms the structure and meaning of a whole new world, a world new in consciousness, a world in which time is the blooming place of real freedom, of real hope, of real humanity. In a word, the new creation, to the extent that it is a reality in our lives, takes place in a new spirit. It takes place, concretely in a new capacity for and quality of vision, experience and action in which we experience ourselves and our world differently out of a new quality of consciousness and thus come to act out of a transformation which transcendently renews the whole of our life from within. In this way, then, those who share in this same Spirit (drink of the one Spirit) constitute a new "body," a body not made of flesh, physical, but a body constituted in and out of spirit. This is a unique kind of body indeed, a place where Jesus dwells and acts in the world. But that location and action take place within the immediacy of the new Spirit. And this transformation into the renewed Body of the Christ is, in the last analysis, what the "new creation" is all about; it is all a matter of Spirit.

While we are still using rather traditional Biblical and theological language, we might translate this reflection into the language which has become common since the twelfth century and speak here of a deeper meaning for "transsubstantiation." The context in which this language came into existence and use was quite restricted: the problem of whether what was on the altar was bread or the body of Christ. Today, we consider this problem in a broader context, that of the presence of Jesus and its meaning in and for the worshipping community itself. And the "substance" in question is not simply a matter of the reality or appearance of bread. The substance in question is the worshipping community itself and the critical question of the Eucharist is the question of *truth:* Is this community in truth the body of Christ? And, in the light of our reflection on the meaning of the new creation, we can see that this truth, the truth or lack of truth in our being baptized into one body in the one Spirit, is the governing consideration for our appreciation of the basic reality of the church and of any of the aspects of its sacramental life. Thus, the basic "transsubstantiation" with which we should be concerned is the transforming renewal which takes place in the new creation. For it is in this transformation or the lack of it that the basic truth or falseness of the church resides. If this is true, true in its beginning and true in the on-going life of the Christian community, then the sacramental life of the church is true and consequently laden with the power which that truth has. The new creation is the deeper transformation, the deeper "transsubstantiation" which brings about the reality of the Body of the Christ under the physical appearances of the human community and the human situation. It is distressing almost beyond description to labor to give some meaning to the practice and theology of the Eucharist only to meet over and over with the old question, "Is He really there or not?" The only answer that can be meaningful to that question is that He is "there" on the altar if He is "here" in the lives of the Christian community. More on this in the following reflection, but it serves to bring out the radical importance of the basic transformation of a community of persons into the new creation in the one Spirit in which all are baptized into the one body. For this is the radical truth of the church: if this is true, the rest is true; if this is false, what else is there? Without this Spirit, there is at best some sort of cultural or civil religion, but the meaning which that Spirit is is absent and the whole thing is empty show.

Thus, the new creation is a matter of spirit, the Spirit in our spirit. And it is this Spirit which is the central meaning and truth of our incorporation into the Christ and its sacramentalization in the reality of Baptism. But it is of the utmost importance to realize that when we talk of the *reality* of baptism/confirmation, we are speaking of the actual functioning of that Spirit as the horizon for our spirit. We are speaking of a vision, experience and action which is dominated by the concrete historical shape which that Spirit gives to the reality of God and the risen Jesus in the actual pattern of our lives. If that Spirit does not come into operation within a person's life, we may have some sort of initiation into some sort of community, but we do not have incorporation into the Body of the Christ. We may have some sort of initiation into a church in some social or legal sense, but the heart, the meaning, is gone, and it cannot truly be called the church of the Christ, God's gathering into Christ in the mission and function of their Spirit. Of course, this is drawing the matter in the sharpest possible terms in order to bring out the function of Spirit in the function of sacramental action of the Christian community. In fact, it is not a matter of "is" or "is not"; rather it is a matter of more and less, of the Spirit's being more and less the horizon for the functioning of our spirit in the world. The more the Spirit of Jesus, the Spirit of God, functions as the background, the horizon against which our spirit functions, the more or less is the Christian community true and false, the more and less true and false we are in and to ourselves and others, the more and less true and false we are to the unfailing truth of God. Thus, the basic truth and hence the basic power of our incorporation into the Body

of the Christ is a matter of spirit, the truth of our spirit in the
Spirit, the presence or absence of that quality of life, vision and
experience which bears the fruits of the Spirit. In this sense,
then, we can speak concretely and experientially of the "grace
of Baptism," a grace which is found in the living experience of
our truth in and to the Spirit of Jesus.

It should be apparent, then, that the new creation is not a
matter of some magic moment when the water is poured and
the words are spoken. Rather, the new creation is the entire
process of a life lived (more and less) in Spirit and truth. And
thus the new creation is not a matter of a once-for-all kind of
beginning so much as a constant process of being renewed, as
Paul says, "in the spirit of your mind," in the whole framework
out of which a person lives. Speaking from an experiential point
of view, we cannot speak of any a priori permanence to the
vocation which being a new creation puts into a person's life
in a way that is more or less clearly experienced. For being the
new creation depends for its living reality on the transformation
of a person's practical consciousness of his own life in which
the question of what one can or will do about one's self finds an
answer in the experience of being freed from the ineluctable
processes of the past and finding in the experience of this
liberation a real opening to the possibility of living a deeply
and truly human existence. And the only way in which we can
experience our own time as the place where this freedom can
really come into existence is through the actual liberation of
our pursuit of being human which takes place in our experience
of the fruits of the Spirit of Jesus in a community where those
fruits bloom in love, joy, peace, goodness, faithfulness to one
another and so on.

The experience of the new creation, then, is a constant beginning, a beginning which takes place to the extent that the
event of the liberation of new hope takes place in our lives as
the Spirit of Jesus becomes the personal and corporate context
out of which we live. It is only in this way that new creation
can be a meaning-filled reality in our lives as we experience

them. For the Christian vocation is a human vocation, the calling and gathering which God brings about within the framework of our human experience. And to be a real vocation, a calling, an invitation—and not merely another "natural" process loaded with the dead predictability of a relentless kind of sameness—this vocation must be a vocation which opens up to our vision and experience the possibility of a real *creativity* within this calling. To live out of a "program," whether that program be the inflexible confines of an imposed regime from some outside force or those of our own self-imposed staleness is the death of the human and the death of any meaningful framework for Christian existence. The question which our consciousness is—"What can we do about ourselves?"—is answered in a word: nothing. It all happens according to the established plan. Nothing new, nothing surprising, freeing is going to happen. Time is something we just live out. Freedom is at best a theoretical human quality, without a history, without a concrete experiential content. And hope is merely a passive waiting for the inevitable to take place. But to live out of the new creation means to live out of liberation from all of this. It means that our consciousness is of an existence that is truly in our hands to grow and expand as we become more and more spirit. It means that our time is a time for freedom, for creativity, responsibility, for owning more and more of our lives as ever new possibilities are revealed to us. It means that our freedom is real, concrete, a historical fact, because of the liberation which the Spirit of Jesus brings about in our life. It means that our hope is deep and rich in the possibilities of truly becoming—ourselves, this in a truly free and creative way.

The absolutely critical importance of a genuine Christian community for the experience of the new creation should be obvious from all we have seen. For the principle factor in the experience of liberation which grounds our experience of being a new creation in the Christ is the unconditioned and permanent commitment which the Christian community makes to the one who is baptized. For it is only in and through this abiding human commitment that we can actually have some experience of the unfailing fidelity of God's love for each and every human person. For the Spirit in which we are baptized into the one Body is a Spirit of love—of God's love for each person, an absolutely faithful and unfailing love, a love which remains in the face of all our rejection. But that love can only enter our experience in the human commitment which a Christian community makes to a person to be there faithfully in love as the context for the person's growth in the life of spirit. It is a Spirit of patience, kindness, gentleness—but perhaps most important of all, a spirit of faithfulness, of pledging our fidelity to one another and living out that pledge in our mutual love, our mutual constant forgiveness. We can see how it is this Spirit in our spirit which reveals what is perhaps the most difficult thing for so many of us to believe in any living and functional way— that it is good for me to be me. It is this seemingly simple act of faith which liberates within us a truly human consciousness, a consciousness which accepts our lives as deeply worthwhile, valuable, good. But without the context of a loving, affirming, faithful community it is hard to see how anyone can make a fundamental and critical initial act of faith in the goodness of their own life. Once again, it is all a matter of spirit, of truth, of faithfulness to spirit and truth.

It is against this background that we can reflect on the concrete significance for our own experience of some of the baptismal themes of the New Testament. We have concentrated our reflection already on the theme of the "new creation" which is brought about by being baptized in one Spirit into the one Body. This focus for our reflection can be deepened by a reflection on the meaning of the water, the word, the dying and rising, the Spirit, fire and judgment and the priestly consecration—all of which fill out the concrete meaning of the new creation in Jesus, the Christ.

The Water and The Word

In the letter to the Ephesians, we find an allusion to baptism as it is connected with the death of Jesus, a death which is an act of love as He handed Himself over on behalf of the bride, the community which He loves. In doing so, Jesus made his bride, his community, holy "having cleansed her by the washing of water with the word, so that he might present the church to Himself in splendor, without spot or wrinkle or anything of the sort, so that she might be holy and without blemish" (5:25–27). The bridal relationship between Jesus and the Church certainly stresses the love which Jesus has for those who are baptized into the one Body and the cleansing with water and the word certainly brings to mind the liturgy of baptism. As a matter of fact this particular passage was used as a "proof text" for Jesus' institution of baptism as a sacrament. But there is more to this passage than a casual or polemic glance would show. It has a strong resonance with another washing in water and word which Ezekiel presents in his presentation of the relationship between Jahwe and Israel. In a touching image of the origins of Israel, Ezekiel speaks of Israel as a new-born baby, born without any future and left in the desert to die (c. 16). She is not cleaned and wrapped up like a child for whom there is love and care; she lies in the desert, abandoned, "weltering in your own blood" (vv. 6, 9). But the Lord passed by and saw her and spoke to her in her very abandonment and the word which is spoken is a command, "Live!" (v. 6). Here is a small insignificant people whose existence is not due to a divine founder like the great pagan cities around her. Her very life is a gift from the compassion of the Lord who calls her to life in the midst of her insignificance. And as she grows, the Lord washes her of her blood, and adorns her to be His own bride, His very own people. The water and the word are not a mere cleansing, they are a life-giving command and a bath which brings something beautiful and lovable into existence because God loves her. And like Israel of old, the "little flock" which is the church owes whatever life or beauty there is in her to this life-giving command and to this life-giving bath into which she is immersed.

This theme of the life-giving word and the life-giving bath complement our consideration of the life of the Christian as a new creation. It emphasizes the fact that this new creation is the work of a love and mercy which form the context for a new beginning, a beginning of life rather than a relentless movement toward death and insignificance. But here as elsewhere we must ask what this means concretely in terms of human experience. Where in our experience do we or can we hear that life-giving word "Live!" and where are we plunged into that life-giving bath. From all that we have seen of the meaning of the resurrection of Jesus, we can see that it is in that event that we are called to a new life, a life rich in hope, a life which really is life and not death masquerading as life. For it is the risen Jesus that God has called us to a newness of life. But it is essential to keep in mind the fact that the meaning of that resurrection is a reality which is borne by Spirit, the Spirit of Jesus, the Spirit of God as that Spirit reaches out to and transforms our spirit, our vision, our experience, our action. It is in that Spirit that the word which God speaks in raising Jesus from the dead— "Live!"—reaches into our life, our spirit to bring its powerful meaning about in our lives and experience, calling us to the true life which is given for us in the risen Lord. But, once again, Jesus is only Lord *for us* in that Spirit. It is only to the extent that that Spirit becomes the background for our vision, experience and action that Jesus is concretely Lord in anyone's life in any real, historical, experiential way. And it is only to the extent that this Spirit is effectively shared among the community that new hope, new vision, new freedom, a new consciousness can bring into our lives the creative command of God, "Live!" Baptism, to the extent that is a reality, is a call to life, but that call to "live" only reaches into our lives in concrete and experiential reality to the extent that the quality of life of the Christian community in fact forms a context for truly living in a truly human way. Life, the life-giving word, the call to life—it is all a matter of Spirit and truth, the Spirit of Jesus bearing witness within our spirit that we are in truth, in faithfulness to our own and each other's very humanity, the free-born children of God, born free to be human in an authentically creative way.

It is all very fine to speak in these terms of life, freedom, creativity, the call to live, to be human. But once again, we must ask what this means concretely and experientially. This brings our reflection to a very familiar theme in the understanding of the reality of baptism. And this is the theme of death and resurrection. It is often pointed out that one of our difficulties in understanding the meaning of the resurrection of Jesus is that we ourselves do not have an actual experience of death and consequently cannot have any experience of resurrection. And this is true. We have not gone through the personal and physical trauma of death. But that does not mean that we cannot have some concrete and experiential understanding of the *meaning* of these realities. For the meaning of death, at least, is far more than the physical experience of the end of life as we know it in physical terms, the weakness, the growing darkness, the loss of contact with the familiar world around us, the coma, the end. Death is more than a physical phenomenon; it is something we *do* personally. And in these terms, there is a *quality* to our dying, which is an act of a living person, just as there is a quality to our living. There is a way of living and a way of dying. And, in personal terms, dying is our ultimate human act of transcendence, of moving beyond the limits of human existence into *terra incognita,* a place whose only chart is the complete set of contradictions which Paul offers us in his description of the resurrection of the dead (I Cor 15:35 ff.). What happens there or in the passing nobody really knows. We symbolize the ultimate seriousness of our lives with the themes of heaven, hell, purgatory, judgment. But the radical Christian hope, though it makes frequent use of these symbols, is that dying is a passage to an imperishable life, that the future to

which we look even beyond death is already guaranteed by
the Spirit of Jesus, the pledge of what is to come. Thus, though
we may have no direct physical experience with death itself, we
can and must see that event and its consequence is some continuity with personal process which we can (and should) experience in the ordinary pattern of our lives. And it is in this
light that we can speak of the meaning which death and resurrection can have in terms of our experience of our own human
processes.

Dying and Rising

In this context, then, we can approach Paul's presentation
of what the new creation is in the creative call to life which the
functioning reality of baptism should be in the life of the
Christian. Speaking to the Romans of the strength of the work
of Jesus in our salvation, he stresses the fact that God's love
for us in Jesus is not based on our deserving, but on a love
which is directed toward us precisely as sinners. Whatever condemnation we might merit for our sins, God's response has
been in Jesus, a response of love that is greater than sin and
evil, a free gift greater than any offense (5:15), a grace far
more abundant than our sinfulness (5:20). This is the source
of Paul's (and the Christian's) hope (5:1-11)—perhaps too
much hope. Paul foresees the problem which would later occasion the preaching of Pelagius. Should we continue to be sinful so that God's grace might even be more abundant (6:1)? By
no means, he answers, because the Christian has died to sin, so
how can he continue to live in it? And this death is a death
which is brought about when we are baptized into Jesus, the
Christ (6:3). For it is a baptism into a death, the death of
Jesus, a burial with Him, so that we might walk in a "newness
of life" just as Jesus was raised from the dead (6:4). So that
just as Jesus died once and for all to sin and now lives for
God, we should consider ourselves as dead to sin and live for

God in Jesus, the Christ (6:11). We have all heard this again and again. But we know at the same time that neither Paul, the Romans nor ourselves have died that once-and-for-all kind of death. Only a few pages later Paul tells us that the good that he wants to do he does not do and the evil that he does not want to do he does (7:19). And we can all say a hearty "Amen" to that. In this, as elsewhere, Paul's "is" is really a "should be"—we should be the body of the Christ, we should be dead to sin, we should be many things which in fact we are not as yet.

It becomes apparent, then, that as idealistically as Paul speaks of the Christian's dying and rising with Jesus, this is not a once-and-for-all reality in our lives. Rather, it is the pattern in which we respond to the creative word of God— "Live!"—as this word calls us to life, to more life, more spirit, more being. But how is it that we can think and speak of ourselves as dying and rising (or anything else) "in Jesus, the Christ"? From all that we have seen in our reflection on the meaning of the Christ and the new creation, we can see that this is a matter of spirit which comes about as we are baptized into the one body in the one Spirit. To "be in the Christ" is to be anointed with the same Spirit which anointed Jesus. And concretely and experientially this means that the background out of which we live, the concrete character of our vision, our experience of ourselves, our world, our personal and corporate history, the context out of which we actively live our lives in decision and engagement, in a word, the concrete horizon for our lives is the Spirit of the risen Jesus. And the actual experiential pattern in which that Spirit functions within the structure which is the human spirit, is the pattern of dying and rising with and in Jesus, the Christ. The new creation, then, takes place within this pattern, this process of death and resurrection in Jesus. But once again, what does this mean in concrete and experiential terms?

In attempting to come to some concrete understanding of what this dying and rising means we immediately run up against the fact that we have already noted, that we have no experience of death and consequently have no personal experience of what resurrection means. But this does not keep any of us from thinking about it, wondering and talking about it. For we all know that this is something that will happen to us, something that we all must eventually do. And thus we look ahead at the experience and interpret it out of our conviction of what life is all about. Thus, for the person who is convinced that there is no meaning, no ultimate or absolute value to living, dying is simply the final absurdity, the final thing that overtakes a senseless and directionless existence. It is just the end. For those whose practical theism gives life a base of meaning and value, dying is what ultimately sanctions all of our decision and action. It is the final act of transcendence which moves us from the limits of this familiar territory in which we live to that "unknown land" which is the life which is yet to come. And for Christian faith dying is the entry into the promise which the risen Jesus brings into human existence through the mediation of His Spirit. It is the entrance into being alive with God and for God in the way Jesus is alive with and for God. This "end" to human life is, in fact, the dawn of a life in which the past life is prelude. Dying becomes the final act of emptying one's self out to God in faith, hope and love, an emptying which opens out to a life whose only paradigm is the raising up of Jesus (Phil 2:8). But what is important is the fact that the Christian's dying is the culmination of a whole life of an "emptying of self" in faith, hope and love in which the resurrection has already been a part of Christian experience. The final act of transcendence, the final transcendence of the human condition as we know it, is an action which is already prepared in the whole pattern of the life of the Christian. And in this sense, the pattern of death and resurrection is experienced in the dying and rising which takes place time and again within the experience of the Christian in the very human processes of transcendence. And, in this sense, the meaning, the concrete meaning of the new creation, of the answer to the creative summons to "Live!" are found in what we have considered and described as the human process of transcendence, a process which is the whole concrete and experiential content of being-spirit.

The description of the human process of being-spirit as a process of death and resurrection brings out a very important aspect of the experience of being-spirit. From all our reflection on the reality of spirit and human transcendence as the concrete and experiential meaning of our belief in God, we might think that it is a simple process which we simply go through. All we have to do is transcend. But there is more to it than that. For human transcendence really involves an experience of dying. We might think of dying as a simple and inevitable biological process. It is simply something that happens. But there is far more to dying. Pretend as we might, we know in a deep though sometimes implicit way that death is an enormous personal event. And since it is a personal event, it is loaded with anxiety for us. And the reason for this anxiety is the fact that we really do not know what lies on the other side of the process. It is truly *terra incognita,* the unknown land. It is easy for us to move into new places when we have them charted out for us in advance. We can move confidently into a place whose configuration, at least in some general way, is already familiar, a place where in a sense we are already "at home." But in a strange land, every corner, every rise in the land can conceal either delight or disaster. To change the metaphor, we are standing with our feet solidly planted in mid-air; there is no certainty, no solidity or security in our posture. And what produces the anxiety in this situation is the fact that, whether we like it or not, whether we admit it or not, we are egotistical people. We are safe and secure within the limits of the place where personal history has brought us and we want to protect what we have found, what we have achieved, what we have become. But as we look into the unknown that lies before us, we can only see nothing, nothing familiar or homey and maybe nothingness for ourselves. And at this every fiber of who we are recoils. And this is true not only of the final kind of physical death we must all eventually face, it is just as true of the little kinds of dying we must all do if we are to be faithful to the structure and the call that the reality of spirit is in our lives. There is an experience of dying which is available to us, then, and this within the very pattern of living. And that experience is, as it were the negative pole against which our experiences of transcendence take place. For that dying is a process of leaving the comfortable and familiar places of our own egoism, the loss of its familiar limits in order to enter into a new context for our personal or corporate human reality.

The experience which is being described is an aspect of the experience of love. For love is not egotistical; quite the opposite, love is directed toward an "other" precisely as an "other." The clearest instance of this is, of course, our understanding of the love of God. There is a thing which some people call love and which the Greeks called *philia:* liking something or someone because that someone or something is like us. Like appeals to like. But this is not what we have learned of God's creative love. If God's love for us were a *philia,* God would base His love on our holiness, our fidelity, our perfection. But the fact is that God's love for us is not that kind of love. For the love of God is directed toward our "otherness" from God in the very fact that He loves us "while we were yet sinners" (Rom 5:8). God's love is *agape,* a love which is not egotistical but a selfless gift of one's self to one who is completely "other." Looking at this from the point of view of our own egoism, we are surprised and call it an emptying of the self for the sake of the one who is loved—a *kenosis* (Phil 2:7). And this is the image of love which Jesus commends to us, to lay down our lives for our friends, a command which Paul takes up in his exhortation that we have the same mind as Jesus, subjecting ourselves to one another as Jesus loves the church, handing himself over for it, emptying Himself of divinity to the very death of the cross. This kind of love, real love, involves a dying. It forms a pattern on our love of one another in which our love is not based on the real or projected likeness between ourselves and others, but is rather based on their utter difference from us in the individuality of their own lives. It is even an essential aspect of our love of our own selves, which cannot be based on the comfortable stability of one particular stage or aspect of our lives, but must be based on the "otherness" which emerges from the changes in us. We love each other not simply for who we are, but far more for who we can and will be. Our love must stand open before the mystery that each of us is and commit us not just by liking what is there but loving what can and will be there. A love which focuses on only one aspect or one stage of a person's history, be that someone else's or our own history is not love at all. It is a fixation. Real love is based on the "more" that we are all called to be, if we are to be really human, really spirit.

We can begin to see, then, how the love which is the very soul of Christian life involves a process of "dying." It involves a constant transcending of the limits of our own existence, our own relation to ourselves and to others. Real love reaches out to something which must always change if we are to be ourselves or if others are to be themselves. And it demands that we die to the limits which we set to our appreciation of ourselves or of others. And the reason why this is a "dying" and not simply a change is our own egoism, the drag which we all experience between the call to transcendence which we are as humans and the very clear desire we all have to remain in comfort, security. The human process of transcendence is not an easy process, but it is a process into which we must constantly enter nonetheless.

Thus, the experience of the new creation involves the experience of "dying." But there is more to it than that. For the "dying" of which we are speaking is a "dying in Christ," i.e., in the spirit of Jesus, the Christ. And this makes an important difference. For this is not a dying in general, or a dying and rising to any old thing. It is a death to every limit and obstacle which impedes the flowering of the Spirit of Jesus in our spirit, in the fruits of that Spirit, in the characteristics of unity, holiness, catholicity and apostolicity which make up the Christian's experience of himself in his world. This is a dying with a direction, with a purpose: to rise with and in Jesus, the Christ. And it is that purpose and direction which gives a ground of meaningfulness to the process of dying. One does not simply die for its own sake, but one dies to one set of limits because of one's faith that beyond that death there lies a "newness of life."

What this means more concretely is that our capacity to go through the process of the transcending of one framework for our vision, our experience, our action, depends for its meaning on our conviction that beyond this present structure for our life there lie real new and richer possibilities. But, as we have seen in our reflection on the realism required for genuine hope, this vision of a "newness of life" lying beyond the "dying" we must do can only be realistic to the extent that our previous movements of transcendence have passed over into horizons which are loaded with meaning and value, human meaning, human value. Our hope depends for its realism on the fact that our previous acts of transcendence have in fact been events of real liberation, the freeing of our spirit for more life, more humanity. It means that those events have freed us to be more and more ourselves as the new stages of our personal or corporate development reveal themselves and make their demands on us. And in this very concrete way we become more and more ourselves, more and more spirit.

It should be noted that there is no program which can plan out and describe this in much detail for us. It is something which we must learn in the very process itself. It is difficult, if possible at all, to specify in very much detail precisely what we are to become. We can see some of it in the description of the fruits of the Spirit of Jesus as this blossoms within human life— in love, joy, peace, patience and understanding, in faithfulness to one another. But precisely how each of us will be each of these is not easy, probably not possible to predict. It is far easier to come to know what we shall not be, as we find out in our own lives and the lives we share what in fact interdicts the human among us. But who we will actually be only emerges as the event of spirit takes place over and over in our lives. So certainty is not the point. The point is hope, a vision of our future as meaningful, worthwhile, filled with humanity, a vision based on the experience of having grown into more and more humanity. And the critical point is the realism of that hope, whether it is based on actual experiences of liberation of more humanity within us or whether it is more wishful thinking or illusion.

Of course, we can all think of examples of people who have so conquered the negativity of their whole personal environment that their development in humanity itself is a kind of miracle. But to plan on these miracles is foolhardy. For the realism of any hope in any humanity depends on a whole human context for its validity. And this means that if we are to hope realistically in the fact that a newness of life opens up for us as we pass through the "dying" of the continuing process of transcendence, we must share in the community of deeply human spirit. It means that no man is an island, that every person who languishes without hope is a judgment on the quality of spirit of the human community in which that person must live. Once again, the functioning and experiential reality of Christian baptism is a matter of spirit—of a continuing and hopeful process of self-transcendence which continually opens us up to deeper and fuller dimensions of humanity itself. But it can only be this against the background of a community which shares, both actively and passively, the Spirit of Jesus, the risen One. For it is in these processes of transcendence, in the dying to one spirit and the rising to a new spirit, that the living reality of the death and resurrection of Jesus enter into the fabric of the human in any concrete and experiential way.

In one spirit, we are all baptized into one body. And that baptism is a baptism into a new creation whose experiential pattern is that of dying and rising with and in Jesus, the risen Lord. And that dying and rising takes place in the context of

the Spirit of Jesus as that Spirit reveals ever new horizons for
our spirit, for newness of life in a very concrete and experiential way. This gives us some initial appreciation of the positive
concrete meaning of Christian baptism. But there is more. Our
reflection until now has focused largely on the positive side of
that meaning in terms of the processes of human transcendence.
But the preaching of the meaning of the risen Jesus and the
meaning of dying and rising in Him and with Him has a
negative pole out of which it is meaningful, the context of
human sinfulness in terms of which Christian baptism is not
only a baptism into the body of the Christ but is a baptism
which leads toward the "forgiveness of sin." This significance
is brought out most explicitly in the sermon which is put in
Peter's mouth in the Acts of the Apostles (2:14–40). In the
face of the amazement of the people of Jerusalem at the
ecstasy of the disciples of Jesus and their miraculous preaching, Peter explains that this event is the fulfillment of the
promises made through the prophets that the Holy Spirit
would be poured out on mankind in the "last days." And this
outpouring of the Holy Spirit is *the* sign by which all the house
of Israel would know that God has raised Jesus, whom they
crucified, from the dead and made Him Lord and Christ. The
people are stunned and ask what to do. Peter tells them to
repent and be baptized in the name of Jesus, the Christ for
the forgiveness of their sins and that they would receive the
gift of the Holy Spirit. Of course, this is all depicted in the
time-sequence within which Luke frames his presentation and
interpretation of the meaning of the resurrection of Jesus. And,
in that context, it is associated with the event of Pentecost some
fifty days after the resurrection.

John's gospel presents the same theme but in a different
time-sequence. For John, the hour of Jesus' "being raised up"
is found on Calvary. It is the hour in which Jesus prays for the
glory which is His as Son (17:1–5). Jesus' last act on the cross
is quite explicit, "he bowed his head and handed over the
Spirit" (19:30). In His death, Jesus fulfills the meaning of
Passover (19:36; Ex 12:46). After these events, John sees a

whole new creation taking place, emphasizing that Jesus' manifestation of Himself is on the "first day of the week" (20:1, 19). And take the opening lines of Genesis, the Spirit of God broods over the scene. This is a Spirit whose outpouring was the sign for Israel of the coming of the last days, the final judgment of God. Now Jesus comes to bring that fulfillment. He brings it in the word *shalom,* peace, which presents Jesus as the One who bears the fulfillment of all of God's promise. And the last fulfillment is in the gift of the Spirit, the Holy Spirit, "whose sins you shall forgive, they are forgiven" (20:21–23). The new creation takes place in the resurrection of Jesus and the meaning and power of that new creation are borne into human history by the gift of the Spirit of God for the forgiveness of sins. Paul presents this same significance for baptism in his characterization of "dying and rising" with Jesus as a death to sin and being live for God (Rom 6:6–11). It is abundantly clear that baptism is for the forgiveness of sins. But once again, we must ask the question of what this means in the life and experience of the Christian when baptism is a functioning part of our human experience.

Forgiveness of Sin

It should be clear at the very outset that this is not an experience of the definitive absence of sin from our lives. Paul's testimony is clear on this point, as we have seen. The experience of the primitive church is apparent; Paul's concern shows the presence of patterns of life which even the pagans found degrading (I Cor 5:1). And any serious and honest reflection on the history of the church, on our own personal history, show us quite quickly that we experience quite clearly the power and guilt of sin in our own lives. The problem is to determine what we mean by this symbol of "sin," and in that light what the experience of forgiveness is in the functioning of the experience of the new creation.

For better or for worse, "sin" has taken on the rather

legalistic meaning of the violation of law. This is probably unavoidable, because religious experience is not simply a personal matter. It is also a social reality and as such tends to organize itself into definite patterns of social existence—creed, cult and code. And even on the personal level, we organize our own religious experience, our own attitudes toward and handling of the absolutes and ultimates which give form and meaning to our existence into a kind of personal creed, cult and code, and our "sins" tend to be the violations of the framework for our lives which these realities supply. This is no matter for surprise. It is really a part of the dis-membering and re-membering process within which everything which happens in our lives takes place. There is no such thing as a "pure experience." Every human experience takes place within the identity (personal and corporate) which forms the framework for the meaning of any experience, whether it is a good or bad experience, thrilling or terrifying, pleasant or unpleasant. And that "identity" is a memory, an active incorporation of present events into past experience which gives a personal interpretation to whatever happens. Take a crude example, eating a raw sheep's eye. When the sheep's eye arrives at dinner, surmounting a heaping tray of rice and the Western guest of the sheikh is invited to the honor of eating the sheep's eye, the guest, if he is a born and bred Westerner, will recoil with revulsion and if politeness wins out over revulsion, he will swallow the eye with the fond hope that it will stay swallowed. A visiting sheikh, on the other hand, will savor it with gusto, with much loud smacking of lips. The same eye, the same physiological process, but two completely different experiences. For one man it is an outrageous thing, for the other a cherished and delightful tradition. We are all creatures of traditions and those traditions form the framework for the interpretation of our experience. It is this memory which judges what happens in our lives, whether it be an ancient memory or a new memory born out of the reaction to or revolt against older *memories of older people*. Thus memory with its creeds, its codes, its cults, doth make sinners of us all, at least in the legalistic sense of the word. For we do not always measure up to our own or anyone else's codes. No matter what vision the experience of the past offers us for the project of the future, we find ourselves failing to realize that vision. We are sinners, religious sinners, cultural sinners, social sinners.

But there is a deeper human reality involved in the reality we symbolize by the name of "sin." And "sin" is a symbol. What it means literally is to miss a target, to throw or shoot something and miss the mark. And in this symbol, we express our own failure and failures to lead lives which head unfailingly to the mark which our vision furnishes us in terms of specific action or of long-range goals. But underlying any Christian or any other vision, cutting through every project we see or foresee, there is the basic human project in terms of which all the rest is finally meaningful. And it is here that what we express by the symbol of "sin" emerges not simply as a failure here or there in the implementation of any religious, cultural or social project, but as an abiding and mysterious reality which cripples such of our pretense toward final liberation, once-and-for-all salvation, even any doctrinaire kind of human optimism. A sense of sin is a sense of the discouraging weakness in our vaunted human autonomy, the experience which tells us that in spite of our "freedom to be human," which results from the "death of God," we are not, in fact, all that free. The "death of God" established, at least for the optimists, the resurrection of the human. But for anyone who reflects on his own experience, it is obvious that this is a very theoretical resurrection, for we experience death at work, gnawing away at the freedom we so passionately seek. The experience is there for anyone who is honest enough to confront it. And perhaps it is because of our sinfulness that so few are really willing to look at this death which lurks at the depths of life.

We are at the rock bottom of human experience and existence here. For we are dealing with the two most powerful forces within our experience, the two poles of experience around which the whole pattern of our lives revolves. Life and death: the two most primary foci of our existence—the experience of being alive (at least biologically) and the absolute certitude of death to come. And it is here that that deeper kind of sinfulness resides, in the struggle between these two gigantic forces. We want to live, but we know that we will die. We want to live life, freely, creatively, joyfully, but we find ourselves living death, buried by the pressures of an "outside," driven to the ground by the urge toward conformity, security, and we are robbed over and over of our joy. With Paul, we know very deeply that "death held sway from Adam to Moses" (Rom 5:14) and far beyond. And this does not just mean that people died; it means far more. It means that all the meaningfulness of human life lies under constant interdict from that force, deep *within* all of us, which refuses life, real life. We have already reflected on the meaning of death and resurrection in biological and personal terms. In that reflection, our attention focused on the positive pole of that process, the process of coming to life, and we have seen this process as a constant process of transcendence. Here our attention is focused on the negative pole, on the force within us which makes coming to life so difficult, even impossible. What is our "sin," our "death"—what does this mean in concrete and experiential human terms?

If death were simply a biological fact, we would not fear it. If that's all there is, "eat, drink and be merry," "break out the booze and have a ball." What we dread is not a biological fact, but a death which robs us now and will rob us eventually of any meaning or value for our lives, an irrational death which, in the last analysis, says to us here and now that we are of no meaning, no value. We have a symbol for that irrational and meaningless existence, too: hell. Hell and its pains are a symbol which capture our dread of ultimate, absolute and irremediable absurdity and insignificance. They express our deep terror at the prospect of "nothingness." But, as we have seen, we have no experience of any absolute—absolute meaning or absolute insignificance and meaninglessness, absolute reality or absolute nothingness. We only experience these absolutes against the backgrounds of the death, the meaninglessness, the insignificance which invade our lives in their day-to-day pattern. And hell is something which we can understand symbolically because it is a reality which we experience in a relative and limited way here and now in the death which gnaws away at everything we call life here and now.

But the existence of this "death" at the depth of life is not sinful. This is just a fact, a "given" of our human condition. The reality of our "sin" and our "sins" emerges in *the way we deal with this fact*. This is where, in the last analysis, we "miss the mark." And there are two ways of dealing with this fact. One way is to avoid it, to ignore, suppress or flee from this all-pervading reality in our lives. We can just pretend that it is not there, that we are not really that way. We pretend that there is no death in us, that our freedom is absolute, unlimited. There is no darkness in us, only light; there is no wrongness in us, only right. It is interesting (not to say tragic) to see what happens when we do this. The fact is that this is a pretense, an illusion, because anyone who is honest must admit that in spite of this pretense, the darkness, the wrongness, the un-freedom remain. But now, instead of being clear forces which we can face honestly and deal with consciously, they take on a demonic character, the character of forces which are at work within us, but which we push into the shadow gloom of the "unknown," the mysterious, and as such they take on an ir-resistible fascination for us. They become a "secret" depth of our spirit, and a demonic point of view out of which we see ourselves and our world. And so we see these things, death, hatred, sex everywhere. But instead of being "facts of life" they are everywhere else the way they are in us, secret, hidden, protected, things to be defended at all costs. They take on that strange mixture of terror and fascination which make us at once flee from them and at the same time seek them every-where. We become utterly preoccupied with them while we exteriorly profess that they are merely "matters of fact." And here is the *Lebenslüge,* that deep living lie which we become. And the inner lie leads to the outer lie. We lie to ourselves that we are not sexed, not angry, not hungry, and out of this lie conceal, disguise, all of this under the mask of "matters of fact." And we come to work out our sex, our anger, our hunger in a way that isolates us from one another in postures of defense and self-protection in which the self is not our real self but a wall of masks by which we hide and protect ourselves from ourselves and anyone else. Isolation, alienation, self-deception, deception of others, defense from ourselves and defense from others, walls around walls around walls. Illusion.

We must start from this depth within us, if we are to come to any concrete understanding of the "forgiveness of sin." For forgiveness lies in the other way, the way of knowing, admitting and living with who we really are. Forgiveness begins with confession, confession first and foremost to our own selves and confession to one another that we are sinners. The way to life, to love is not around death, but *through it.* If the cross of Jesus means anything at all for us, it means this: that Jesus did not bypass or skirt death to arrive at life, but that He came into life *through death,* down, into and through death. If forgiveness is to begin, it must begin by living with the "death" that lies within us, not by fighting it. And this is the great Christian, the great human paradox—it's not matter of the way out of death, it's a matter of the way in, into death. It is a matter of being able to come to live with death, the crippled freedom we all are and have, the powerful forces of sex, identity, fear, aggression and so on which form the iceberg whose tip alone emerges in our public lives, the lives we live publicly with our own selves and with others.

The forgiveness of sin, then, is not a matter of an escape from the dark areas of human existence. Rather, it is a matter of transcendence, of transcending the reality of the death that dwells within us, this precisely by entering into that death, owning it, admitting it to ourselves and to one another. And this kind of confession does not erase that power from our lives; it does not make us immortal in any sense of the word. We must still enter into death, into the fact of biological death and into the fact of the dying we must do each day to any falsely idealistic image of who we would prefer to be: someone else. We must die to all the false innocence, the false righteousness, the false perfection which impede any realism in our acceptance of ourselves or of one another. Rollo May has remarked that innocence involved in action cannot avoid murder. And a colleague has wisely said that the greatest enemy of the good is the perfect. So much of our Christian history has shown us how the enthusiasm for perfection cannot tolerate what Marc Oraison calls the "wound of mortality." Forgiveness begins by living with this wound, the wound of emptiness, the wound of death, the wound of imperfection, in a word, with the acceptance of who we really are. Without this acceptance, we can only miss the mark, project some kind of false image of ourselves and insist that "I really am not that way; I really didn't do that." Without this acceptance we have only excuses, excuses, excuses, which is a long way from forgiveness. Without this acceptance, we can only erect false barriers of innocence or perfection which, in the last analysis, only divide us off from our own selves and from one another. Forgiveness can only begin with an acceptance of fact, that fact of the way we really are and the stunning revelation that it is *this* person whom God loves, not some figment of our imagination or pretense.

We can begin to have some concrete understanding of Baptism for the forgiveness of sin when we look at the reality of baptism in these terms. For when Christian baptism is a functioning reality its reality is known in the experience of forgiveness. And the reality of the experience of being a "new creation" does not consist on covering over that darkness which is within us with more darkness. Rather, it is the experience of the transformation of that darkness by the clear, hard light of self-acceptance and mutual acceptance as we really are. It is this kind of honest and realistic acceptance which transfuses the death that we are with life, floods the darkness we are with light. For as deception and pretense die in our honesty with ourselves and one another, a new and stunning hope comes into being—the *realistic* hope that life, that love are stronger than this death and darkness. But that is only possible to the extent that baptism is a commitment, an absolute and unconditioned commitment to one another, to be an unfailing context of acceptance, of forgiveness no matter what. Only this kind of unconditioned fidelity can liberate the realistic hope that in spite of our sin we are and will continue to be loved.

Traditional theology expressed this aspect of baptism, though somewhat negatively, in the doctrine of the "character." Linguistically and culturally, this idea has to do with marking and branding and perhaps many of us still think of this aspect of baptism in terms of some kind of distinguishing mark by which God or the angels or someone else can tell who is Christian and who is not. Of course, none of us experience this "mark on the soul," and we might well wonder whether there is any such thing at all. But there is a sense in which this tradition is meaningful and in which the "character" can be seen to be a part of the experience—indeed a basic and critical part—of being a "new creation." And this consists precisely in the experience of a mutual commitment of Christian to community and community to Christian, the unconditioned and irrevocable mutual commitment which the reality of baptism ought to be. The concrete experiential reality of the "character of baptism" is a commitment which Christians make to one another in the shape of the pledge to love, joy, peace, patience, kindness, goodness, faithfulness to one another, gentleness and self-control. It is out of this lived experience that the "character of baptism" functions as the context for the forgiveness of sin. And more positively, it is out of this lived experience that the "character of baptism" serves as the context for growth toward the Christian, growth toward the human. Once again, it is a matter of spirit, the Spirit of Jesus overtaking our spirit in the pattern of day-to-day Christian existence, day-to-day human existence becoming day by day more Christian, more human. In this way, the "new creation" is the fruit of a "new Spirit," a new vision, a new experience of ourselves and others in our world in the liberation of a radically new hope: the hope that we can in fact be and become ourselves in a freed and creative way, that we can live with the death which is in us and transcend it by passing through it.

To live the experience of Baptism and Confirmation, then, is to be a "new creation." It is a "transsubstantiation," a deep transformation of the substance of our experience of living, a transformation of our consciousness of who we are and what our world is, a transformation of our vision, our experience, our action in the liberation of a radically new hope. That hope is a hope that life is stronger than death, any death, be it the biological terminus of life as we know it or the many deaths we must die in order to really live. But that hope can only escape being wishful thinking to the extent that the members of a Christian community make the kind of unconditioned and faithful commitment to each other which is characteristic of the Spirit of the Lord. The newness is the new and renewing experience of growing freedom, always limited, always partial, always coexisting within our lives with a great deal of unfreedom, but a freedom nevertheless. The newness is the dissolution of the old divisions, the old individuality, individualism, the old separateness and the recovery of a deep and primal unity in which we can feel ourselves bound to others in the context of the on-going process of the forgiveness of sin.

Further, it is an experience of a constant new *creation*. If Baptism is a living reality in a person's life, that life should be experienced as a constant *beginning*. In the beginning was the Word and in the beginning is the Word. The Word gives shape and substance to a world, our world. But that Word, God's Word, "It is good, very good," comes in our beginnings, revealing a world which is not old and stale, but a New World, a world which does not go around and around in the dull repetitions of the past, but a World which is constantly bringing forth the new, the fresh, the new hope, the new vision, the new man. It is a world in which the old, the stale, the repetitious, the ineluctable is "nothing" and the new world is being created, brought out of nothing, out of Egypt into *terra incognita,* an unknown land, but a land full of promise to the extent that we get down on hands and knees and make it blossom with the new promise, the new hope.

Perhaps the simplest way to say it would be to say that, if Baptism is a functioning experience in our lives, we truly experience a living call to be human.

The Body of
the Lord

This is a reflection on Eucharist. "Eucharist" is a translation of the name of a Jewish prayer, the *berrakah,* which was a prayer of praise and thanksgiving offered in the name of the family by the father at the end of the Passover supper, praising and thanking God for the goodness, grace and mercy with which He fills the world. The Christian Eucharist, of course, is a recognition of God's goodness, grace and mercy which are supposed to be present in the community in Jesus, and the praise and thanksgiving which this presence should evoke. But our concern here, as in the rest of these reflections, is a concern for meaning, for the experience of goodness, grace and mercy which rises to expression in the celebration of our Eucharist. We have already devoted some attention to "transsubstantiation" in what seems to be its proper context, namely, the functioning in a person's life. This reflection will center on two main themes, the themes of "body" and "presence," and our question will be: "What does it mean, what is the experience of being 'body' and 'present?' "

This Is My Body

Gearing for Action. We will begin with the experience of being "body." But immediately we encounter a deep and serious problem. The problem has a number of names, dualism, literalism, polarization. But whatever we may choose to name the problem (or whether we even see that there is a problem), the result is the same, and that is that what we mean (our own experience) when we say "This is my body" is meager and impoverished indeed. By and large, we tend to experience ourselves as body in terms of the outer surface of our skin. This is where we begin in terms of the outside and where we end in terms of the inside. Everything on this side is ourselves and everything on the other side is "the world," the "rest" of reality. In these terms, then, being a body mainly has the meaning (the experience) of being separate, distinct from the rest of the world "out there." Being a body is thus an organism and organization for being separate, for being different from and over against the world.

Our experience does not begin this way. We gradually learn that there is a place where we leave off and something else begins. The warm, safe wetness of the womb gives way to another womb in which the blanket, the thumb and the toe are pretty much the same, our body. But bit by bit we learn a difference, the blanket does not respond to our suckings in the same way that our fingers and toes do. All the differences in the suckable things we experience teach us that we are different from the outside and that out there there are differences between the things we can suck. The blanket, the rattle, the squeaky little doll, these are all fine, but they can't hold a candle to the deep warmth of mother's breast which enfolds us and gathers us back to the place we came from. It's bad enough to come from the warm, safe place we start in, to be ripped out, held up by the heels dripping blood and urine, welcomed into this cold, strange place with a smack on the rear. But then we must start to sort this new place out. We've got to get organized—and get organized we do, like it or not. The things we like to suck on—this is not us and away they go. The things we excrete—this is not us and away they have to go. And suddenly we find out that everyone is not the same, and away goes another feeling of oneness. Get organized! And we are off on the road which leads to the constant discoveries of what we are not and what we are, separating ourselves off from what we are not and in this way coming to an awareness of what we are.

Thus it is that we get organized. But what is it that is getting organized? The physical structure of our limbs and organs, given enough nourishment and maintenance, takes care of itself. Where we find ourselves most active in this organizing process, however, is in the area of awareness and vision. As we grow, we gradually learn the concrete relations, attitudes and demands which the world ("out there") imposes on us and which we, in our turn, impose on the world. We develop a kind of double vision, looking out on a very concrete world of people, things, events, structures, but we see all of this in a deeply practical vision. For we do not just see the "outside"; everything we see, we see in terms of what it means to us—we see everything as active people, people on whom what is seen makes all kinds of demands. In this sense, our awareness, our vision is always somewhat narcissistic for we have the obligation not only to organize ourselves in isolation from or in passive contemplation of the world in which we live, but we also have the obligation of organizing the world in this same process. We do not live in *a* world, any old world; we live in *our* world, a world which has a very concrete meaning for us, a world which demands that we adopt very particular personal postures and do very specific things. Thus our world is not just any old place. It becomes a very special personal place brought into being in the process of what we can or cannot do about it, what we should and should not do in it, who we are not and who we are in it. We come to see and experience it in a very particular and personal way and in this way we give it a very particular and personal meaning.

But it is important to reflect on some of the things which have happened in this important, indeed, essential process of organization. Perhaps the most fundamental happening is that from experiencing ourselves as one with our environment, one with the limits of our experience, we have moved to an experience of duality, an experience of not being our environment, of not being the limits of all our experience. We experience two realities, ourselves, our own body "in here," and we experience the world, something which is not us, "out there." And against the background of this kind of awareness, *"this is my body"* comes to mean what is contained within the outer surface of our skin. The rest of what we experience is our "world," *not* our "body." Our awareness of being-a-body has thus become organized to see ourselves as separate and distinct individuals in and from the "world." Perhaps some might have the suspicion that this is something wrong. It is not meant to be wrong. It is precisely this kind of organization of our awareness that makes it personally possible to look on our world as something which can be manipulated to our advantage. It is out of this organization of our consciousness that we can manipulate the forces and materials of the "world" to bring about the achievements of science, technology and art which make human existence and experience less and less brutish. Getting organized is not necessarily Bad News.

The separation of our own body from the world is not the only separation which takes place in the process of getting ourselves organized for the business of living. There is a further separation which takes place within the limits of our own personal reality. In the groping process of learning to find ourselves different and distinct from what surrounds us, every aspect of our experience speaks to us, the soles of our feet, the palms of our hands, the surfaces of our tiny body, the mysterious groanings and gurglings from somewhere inside us. Sounds, movements, fuzzy figures becoming clearer, funny feelings all over, the startling sounds of our own voice—all of these are signs on the road to the discovery and organization of our selves, startling and fascinating experiences which surprise and puzzle us. But familiarity breeds contempt. We get used to these signals. Time to eat. Time to go to the bathroom. Time for bed. The curiosity, the fascination of these feelings and this kind of awareness is lost and our center moves inward and upward. We grow away from our body. Our body becomes an automatic, autonomic "thing" at the service of a "higher principle" —often enough considered to be in our head. Consciousness, awareness, go to our heads and our body becomes another thing among the things which make up a somewhat "outside" world, outside the *real* place where we live—our mind, our soul, our spirit.

Thus, along with the organization of our experience into the twofold experience of "body" and "world," we become organized into "body" and "soul," matter and spirit, mind and members. Some of the enthusiasts of Gestalt psychology lament this second kind of organization. Among other deplorable effects it produces the "head trip," a separation of our thinking and our communication, and our total experience. But this kind of organization is not necessarily all that bad. After all, we should be organized at least to the extent that we no longer experience every aspect of our bodily experience as if it were happening for the first time. There are other things to do than "listen to our bodies." True, it is good therapy, but therapy has a meaning and purpose beyond itself, the business of day-to-day living. One can hardly face a business deal, a classroom situation, a problem in the home with "My stomach tells me . . ." or "My breathing tells me . . ." We will return to this later. The point here is to face the simple fact that in the process of organization for living, the concrete, experiential meaning of "This is my body" gradually shrinks down to that which is divided and separate from the world, divided and separate from the "higher" power of spirit, soul, mind.

But what has happened in this process of organization? Have we brought body and world into being by the process of getting organized? Have we brought matter and spirit, body and mind into being? The answer is obviously "No." What we have done is a matter of organization, the organization of ourselves in relation to our world, the organization of ourselves in relation to ourselves. What we have done is organize our awareness, our consciousness, our attitude, our own system of personal energy in order to confront ourselves and our world so that our personal needs and goals may be accomplished—food on the table, a roof over our head, money in the bank, protection from hunger, privation and pain. We have organized our consciousness and our energies, in Dr. Deikman's terms, into an *action mode*. Physiologically and psychologically we are geared for action, for the very basic and necessary action of achievement and survival. There are all sorts of names for this process, "adjustment" or "conformity" to the "real world," a "sense of reality," "sanity." And this mode of awareness, this consciousness, this "spirit" has its own characteristics; subject is not object, body is not world, matter is not spirit, boundaries between self and world are sharp and clear. Our success and survival depend on distinction and separation. And it is in terms of this mode of organizing our attention and energy that we learn to manipulate, to "handle" ourselves and our environment.

But the point of this first reflection on "body" is what we mean when we say "This is my body" when our attention and consciousness are organized in this active way. And it should be apparent that when we are organized for action, for achievement and protection, we are organized in terms of separateness, of division from the world around us. There is a clear boundary between "in" and "out," "here" and "there," "me," "you" and "it." "This, my body" means the clearly defined limits of the outer surface of our skin; everything inside the skin is me, everything outside the skin is the world of people and things in which but apart from which I do my living. Everything "in here" is geared for action toward the "out there." And, as we have noted repeatedly, this is a fact, a useful and important fact of day-to-day living.

But this is more than a fact. It is also the source of a problem when we come to an attempt to understand what we mean by the "body of the Lord." And the problem arises from the fact that this kind of organization occupies so much of our time and energy in the daily business of striving and coping that we can all too easily say that this is all there is and that this is all we can mean when we say "this is my body." All that body can mean is the body geared for action, the separate, discrete thing made up of nerves, muscles, organs, skin. This becomes *the* reality of body. Whatever else body may mean, it must, in the last analysis be reduced to this level of "reality." This is the one and only "real body." This is the only place where the human person can be; this is the only real organism and organization of human life. Traditionally, this attitude toward body has been called "realism," but there another name for it—if we have the capacity and honesty to stand back from the convictions of Western culture and see it for what it really is—is literalism, the reduction of any possible meaning to one simple level, the level of reality which occupies most of our waking and working attention.

It is this kind of literalism which has produced the kinds of dualism which have plagued Western thought and practice for centuries. The separation of body and spirit has forced some people to make a choice between the two—which of the two is better, more real, more acceptable. And the answer has been, "Spirit is better, more real, more acceptable." And we end up with all those attitudes toward body which make it the object of contempt. The body is the creation of the God of evil (Manicheism); marriage is evil (Encratism); Gratian's celebrated "two kinds of Christians, the real Christian, who vows celibacy, ministers at the altar, and spends the day in prayer and the praise of God, and the rest who, because of their weakness are permitted to marry, till the fields and contribute to the support of '*the* Church.'"

Philosophically, this dualism jelled systematically in the eighteenth century to produce the chasm between subject and object which has challenged reflection on human knowledge ever since. Subject is subject and object is object and never the twain shall meet! Ecclesiologically, it has produced the clear separation of church (body) and world. In is in and out is out and never the twain shall meet! Politically, it has produced the kind of nationalism that says "We is we and they is they and never the twain shall meet"—the paranoia of self-defense, mistrust, arms race, war. Socially, it divides people into have and have-not, couth and uncouth, innocent and guilty—"Surely I am not like *that!*"

And theology has not remained aloof from and uninfected by this kind of literalism, dualism, and polarization. And perhaps the Eucharistic debates between "realists" and "symbolists" are one of the clearest examples of the polarization. Reality is reality and symbol is pretense, make-believe, poetry, invention —and never the twain shall meet. From the bizarre oaths handed to Berengar by Cardinal Humbert in which the "true and catholic faith" maintained that the body of the Lord was in truth and reality (and not *merely* symbolically) broken by the hands of the priest and torn by the teeth of the faithful to the recent debates on transsignification and transsubstantiation, the chasm between the real and the symbolic has proved to be perhaps the greatest obstacle to a theology of the Eucharist which is fruitfully and consistently related to the mysteries of Resurrection and Church. For the "realist" the body of the Lord is a literally physical body, a "real" body which is not a "mystical" body, not a "sacramental" body. How the "real" body is connected with the "sacramental" or "mystical" body is anybody's guess, but somehow it is so that we can worship Jesus who is "really there on the altar" (not here in the faithful or there in the scripture proclaimed).

Literalism, dualism, polarization, all geared for action—is this all there is, the only way we can go? No. There is another way and that is to stand back from the separateness, the divisions and look at the deeper, more primitive and yet more significant unity.

Gearing for Union. If we take the time to reflect on our experience, we will find that our experience of being body contains much more than the experience of separation, distinction from the "world" out there. The separateness is there; there is no denying it. We have organized ourselves, our energies and our vision in such a way that we become able to "handle," to "cope with," the world which has become experientially external to us. Psychiatrists can measure and have measured the characteristics of this body. Striate muscle systems and sympathetic nervous systems dominate physiologically; beta waves sweep the brain; psychologically our attention is obectively focused, our sense of boundaries between ourselves and the other are heightened, shapes and meanings mean more to us and are experienced more clearly than things like color and texture. We are ready for the race, often enough the rat race.

The fact that there is another, a profoundly meaningful dimension of body becomes clear when, in the process of gearing for action, this other dimension is ignored or rejected. For it is precisely when we make up our minds implicitly or explicitly that "reality" is only a matter of manipulation, defense, coping, striving that a little voice somewhere begins to tell us that all is not right. Something is missing. We may or may not have the ears to listen to this voice, but it is there. Eventually it will have its say, one way or the other. Maybe its quiet urgings will speak in terms of a sour taste which all our striving takes on, or maybe in the fatigue, the emptiness which we feel in the midst of it all. Maybe it will speak the louder but more subtle voice of violence, destruction of others, destruction of ourselves. But speak it will, speak it must. And the reason why it must speak out is that it is the voice of a body crying out for life, striving to be born. And that body is the very body of our own humanity. It is not enough to be a machine in a world of machines because we simply are not machines and something must and will cry out within us that we are people and that we simply cannot live like machines. We may ignore that cry, abort that body, strifle that awareness, but we do this at the price of killing our very humanity in the process. And when we remember that all humanity is one humanity, we can see quite clearly that we can kill all humanity when the process is a social, cultural decision.

Is there any way out? Is it possible to transcend, to climb

up and over, to pass beyond the boundaries which gearing for action sets between us and the world, between our self and our body? Is there any escape from the prison to which the dualism and polarization of gearing for action condemn us? The answer is yes. The very fact that the separateness, the dualism and polarization to which gearing for action leads us eventually raise a quiet but persistent question in us shows us that this kind of organization of our personal energies is not the final and completely satisfying answer. That little voice, that stale taste—these are an invitation to us, an invitation to look beyond this kind of organization, to seek after a body which is something other than the narrow limits of our epidermis. We are free to accept or reject this invitation, but it is still an invitation, an invitation to look for more, a "more" which is a deeper and wider experience of ourselves and our world.

But how can we go about discovering this "more"? How can we get out of this trap of individualism, dualism and polarization? One thing should be obvious at first sight. And this is the fact that the organization of our awareness and energy into the striving and coping mode has been brought about by a process of separations. And if we can make ourselves aware of the reality of this process, we can come to realize that this kind of personal organization is not simply "given," an immutable, inescapable fact. This awareness, then, serves to relativize what we have come to see as the "only real world," to indicate that there is another way of organizing our energies, our vision to bring another body into being. Whether or not we choose to follow out this suspicion, to see where it will lead us experientially is a matter of choice. The awareness is an invitation, no more. We can settle for "realism" and reject the "unreal," the "kooky," vision of a broader consciousness, a broader vision. But from what we have seen, it should be apparent that this rejection is one option we have for the organization of our energies and vision. Gearing for action and remaining geared for action, for striving, achieving, coping with the world of other people and things is one kind of self-organization; gearing for union, for opening up our energy into a system of active reception of the world of people and things, into a kind of awareness which sees the deeper unity of ourselves and our world—this is another kind of organization, another kind of body.

The point of all of this is simple, but in all probability it is a difficult point for people like us to accept, living as we do in a culture which defines "reality" in terms of a vision and organization of energy which is so profoundly literalistic and manipulative. But the fact is that some segments of our culture (indeed *scientific* segments as well as the counterculture) have come to see that this is not the only way to define ourselves and reality. One segment of our culture experiences and defines itself in terms of the values and vision of an industrial, nationalistic organization of cultural energies: a buck is a buck; do unto others before they do unto you; whatever it costs, survive in this dog-eat-dog world. Out of this experience and vision, then, "This is my body" has a meager, defensive, literal meaning. But there is another experience, another vision out of which "This is my body" has a broader and more inclusive experiential meaning. And this vision is one which arises out of the adoption of a posture of active receptivity toward the world of people and things in which we live, our own past, present and future and the constant deepening of the experience of unity with ourselves, others and the world itself. Rather than holding the world at arm's length, this vision and experience welcomes all into its consciousness and experience with wonder, love, and a more profound attention to the dazzling richness of our own lives and the world in which we come to live. Rather than defining, shoring up and defending the boundaries of our *ego,* this vision and experience lets go of ego-boundaries and reaches out in love and trust.

We can draw two conclusions from this reflection. The first is that what we mean (see, experience) when we say "This is my body" is a matter of the kind of vision and experience of ourselves and our world which we allow to develop. In other words, it is a matter of *spirit,* the concrete spirit out of which we live our lives. Put in abstract, metaphysical terms, body is constituted by a visible vision. Or, what we see is what we are, and what we are is what we see. And the second conclusion is that the fully *human* body is a body which is constituted by a vision, an experience of one's self and the world (i.e., a spirit) which is geared for union in its active receptivity of one's own past, present and future, of one's fellow humans and the world at large. The fully human body is more than a mere physical body. It is a symbolic body. And this does not mean that we have a make-believe body, but it means that we see and experience ourselves as gathering everything into a profound unity and, at the same time, being gathered into the oneness of everything.

Admittedly, these are hard words for the literalist in all of us. It is difficult for us to accept the fact that we are more than our skin and bones, our own physical body and very individual soul. And to the extent that we cannot or will not accept the fact that we can be more, we are no more. We make ourselves into that kind of island where, when the bell tolls, it tolls for someone else, not me or thee. Further, because of this same kind of literalism, we tend to think and feel that gearing for union is a matter of gearing for physical union, that somehow, we must become more than ourselves physically. We feel that we must somehow recreate our past physically, merge with others and the universe physically. "Reality," in other words, is physical reality. But the fact is that reality is far more than the physical. The startling and paradoxical fact is that, if we let go of this kind of vision, not only does our own reality not melt away but it actually comes into a new and more profound actuality. We find ourselves people of such amazing variety and richness in the past and loaded with such rich and diverse possibilities for the present and the future. In recapturing the profound unity of reality within our own vision and experience, we come to a far more profound experience and appreciation of our own rich uniqueness as well as the uniqueness of everyone and everything else. But the important paradoxical fact is that we cannot arrive at this rich, liberating and deeply transforming vision by hanging on to the boundaries and defenses of the literal vision. We must let go and letting go is very difficult and frightening for all of us.

This is my body. All of it. All of me, my past, my present, my future. All of you, your past, your present, your future. All of it, its past, its present, its future. The bell really does toll for thee and me, all of us, all of it.

The Body of the Lord

The Bread and the Cup. The problem with any reflection on the meaning of the Eucharist arises from the literalism which afflicts all of us as we try to approach any deeper understanding of it. If we try to break through our literalism to a richer understanding, we are almost always faced with the reply, "Yes, but is He *really* there?" And the "really" in the question usually reflects the fear of changing one's point of view from one's traditional devotional and theological attitude. The priest tends to ask whether he really has the power to make Jesus really be there. And we must all know of men who define their priestly ministry primarily in terms of this power. Most of us have heard the traditional sermon at the ordination or first Mass of a young priest in which the preacher rhapsodizes about this young man's new power to bring Jesus from heaven to earth with the words of consecreation. What others mean by the question varies. It can mean, "Is He really there so that I can adore Him?"—or, "If He's not there the way I thought, what have I been doing all these years, all those visits, all those hours of adoration—what do they all mean?" However one would answer these questions, one thing is absolutely fundamental and that is to break out of the literalism with which we have understood and explained the meaning of the Eucharist and recapture the profoundly symbolic realism of eucharistic faith and devotion. And we can make a start by reconsidering what Jesus meant when He said, "Take and eat; this is my body."

For the literal-minded, the "this" which Jesus refers to when He says "This is my body" is a physical reality, the reality of bread. But this ignores the fact of the far richer and broader meaning which the Unleavened Bread has in the context of the celebration of the Passover. And whether or not the Last Supper was in fact a Passover meal, all the accounts of it situate it in a Passover setting, a setting which gives the words and actions of Jesus a far greater depth and breadth of meaning. For in that setting, bread is not just bread and cup is not just cup, but the bread is the Unleavened Bread and the cup is the Cup of Blessing. And here is the great difference between breaking and eating this bread and breaking and eating any other bread. And the difference lies in the spirit, the vision, the experience and hope in which this bread is eaten and this cup is shared. It is in this spirit that the prayer of blessing which accompanied the eating of the bread and the sharing of the cup gives a unique meaning and power to this bread and cup.

Holding the bread in his hand, the head of the family blesses God for the redemption of the people from Egypt, for the privilege of sharing the experience of this holy night, for eating this bread. He utters the hope, alive in this moment, that this people will always share the meaning and power of this night, that this people will continue to be sanctified in the midst of all people and that thus all peoples will come to share in the meaning and power of the deliverance of Passover and worship God with one accord. At the end of the supper, as he held the final cup, the cup of blessing, the head of the family once again blessed God for feeding the world with grace and mercy, for the good and pleasant land into which the people had been led and prayed for God's mercy on His people, on Jerusalem, on God's altar and temple.

The bread and the cup, then, are far more than bread and cup. They are elements of a symbolic action (which is a far cry from a "symbolic gesture"!). And the action is symbolic in two radical senses. It is symbolic in the original sense of the word "symbol"; it is a gathering together of a whole spectrum of common religious experience, a religious experience which gives Israel its very identity as a people. The Passover narratives, blessings and thanksgivings do more than recall a dim and distant past. They actually bring that past (as well as the future of God's promise) into the present. The eye, the mind and the heart of the celebrants are enlarged to see themselves in a profoundly real oneness with the events of Exodus, Sinai, the entrance into the land, the building of Jerusalem, the dedication of the Temple. All of this experience is relived as the bread is broken and eaten, as the cup of blessing is shared. The past, the present, the future are one, are here, living and breathing life into the identity and the hope of the celebrants. All of this is gathered up into the breaking of the bread and the sharing of the cup.

The action is symbolic in a second sense. And this means that it fulfills the function of any symbolic action in human life. It is a bringing into expression of the meaning and values which form the heart of the identity of an individual or a people. The unexpressed soon becomes the irrelevant, the non-functioning. And in this sense, the renewal of the reality of the central events which bring this people into existence is essential to the maintaining of these values in the attention and the life of this people. The great events which form the concrete history of the covenant love between God and His people are renewed and deepened in their celebration.

This, then, is a symbolic reality, nonetheless real for its being symbolic—more real in fact, with a reality which reaches far beyond the physical realities of bread and cup. There is a physical bread and a spiritual bread, a physical cup and a spiritual cup. Beyond the physical realities, there is a deeper and broader reality which comes to these elements from the *spirit* in which their reality is seen, proclaimed and shared. It is that spirit which gives to these elements their gathering and celebrating power, symbolic power—but *real* power, *real* meaning! It is the shared vision, the shared experience, the shared pattern of life within which bread and cup reach out into the past and into the future to make all of the history and hope of Israel *really* present, present with all their liberating and strengthening power. It is in the one spirit, the spirit of Israel bathed in the Spirit of the Lord which gives real meaning, real power, real presence to the concrete events in which God has claimed this people for Himself. It is the same Spirit of the Lord which gives solidity to the hopes of this people for their own future and the future of all men. For this is the unfailing Spirit of the unfailing God whose former love bears the promise of the unfailing pledge to a constant future love. Out of all this comes the spirit, the vision, the experience, the life which gives this bread and this cup their meaning, their truth, their power.

The eating of the bread and the sharing of the cup of blessing, then, is an event of spirit, the Spirit of Israel bathed in the Spirit of the Lord. And it is the Spirit which brings into this moment all the past, the present and the future of God's promise. It is this Spirit which makes of this event the real presence and the real power of the Passover of the Lord. It is in this Spirit that this event has its profound symbolic reality —not a make-believe reality, but symbolic reality, not a literal or physical reality, but a symbolic reality.

It is against this background that the primitive Church remembered, proclaimed and celebrated the action of Jesus when He took up the bread and the cup of Passover. Once again, this is not merely a literal memory recalling physical facts and actions. It is an inspired memory, a memory animated by Spirit, the Spirit which gives to the Christian the ability to proclaim that Jesus is alive, that Jesus is the Lord out of the profound transformation of the human spirit by the Spirit of the Lord. And this is not simply the memory of a man. It is the memory of a man in whom and through whom the Christian sees and knows that God has brought the world and all of human history into a profound new unity, it is a memory of the Lord. And to see the Lord means far more than the vision of a man, even a man in shiny clothes. It means seeing the great final act of renewal and unification which God has finally begun in and through Jesus. And this vision is a vision in the Spirit of the Lord.

Against this background, perhaps, we might be able to see that the Church means far more than bread or cup when, one with the Lord in the one Spirit, it repeats his words, "This is my Body; this cup is a new covenant in my blood." Through the focus of the last supper, the community, one with its Lord, bursts the bonds of Egypt's slavery and cries, "*This* is my body!" It wanders through wild and savage places to enter into covenant love with God and cries, "*This* is my body." It enters into the land of promise, the temple of God's presence and glory and cries, "*This* is my body!" It gazes with wonder and hope at the future of the promise when all men will worship God, when God will be all in all and cries, "*This* is my body!" From the beginning to the end, the past, the present, the future of God and man, all of it, "*This* is my body!" And the cry of the Church is the cry of the Lord, a cry of praise and thanksgiving to God who, in the One Spirit, brings to life the one body. For that one Spirit is the presence of the Lord to His Church, a light to the eyes lighting up everything and everyone with a new reality, a spark of hope, a courage and strength for life constantly bringing promise to fulfillment.

There is a physical bread and a spiritual bread, a symbolic bread; there is a physical cup and a spiritual cup, a symbolic cup, just as there is a physical body and a spiritual body, a symbolic body which is a life-giving spirit. And it is in the spiritual and symbolic bread and cup that the gathering (the symbolizing) takes place, the gathering of past and future of God in the real presence, the gathering of many into the one body of the One Lord in the One Spirit. Once more, perhaps tediously by now, it is all a matter of Spirit, the Spirit of God in His Christ, gathering together the one body. *This* bread, *this* cup—*this* is my body.

From this reflection, it should become clear that the celebration of the Eucharist is a matter of Spirit and truth. It is a matter of Spirit in the sense that a sacramental, a eucharistic vision takes place when our vision, our experience, the whole pattern of our life and hopes are transformed by the Spirit of God, the Spirit of Jesus as the reality and power of the Resurrection penetrate more and more into the fabric of our being. We do not see just Jesus (either the Baby Jesus or the "lonely prisoner of the tabernacle"), but we "see the Lord," which means seeing much more. "Seeing the Lord" is a matter of seeing everything, ourselves, our lives, all of human life and history, in a new way—as transformed in principle and possibility in the fact that God has raised Jesus from the dead and made Him Lord and Christ. It is a vision of a new heaven and a new earth and profound new possibilities for our own lives and the lives of everyone else. The New Spirit bathes our spirit and transforms it and the whole of our lives, giving us a new vision, a new experience, a new possibility for action, as we come to share the fruits of this Spirit in the lives we share.

It is a matter of truth in the sense that the power of the celebration of the Eucharist resides in the truth of its celebration. And the question of truth in this case is the question of whether or not in fact we have all been baptized into one Body in the one Spirit, whether or not in fact all have drunk of the one Spirit. For it is here that the radical transformation, the radical transsubstantiation takes place not merely in the bread and the cup, but in the whole reality and possibilities of human life itself. Is there in fact a new heaven, a new earth? Have we in fact put on the new man, created in God's sight in the holiness and righteousness of God's truth? Are we in fact the new creation, or are we still divided into Jew and Greek, male and female? If we want to look to the power of the Eucharist to bring about its effect, the unity of the one Body, then we should ask ourselves these questions of our truth to the meaning, the reality and power of the Spirit of the Risen Lord in the day-to-day pattern of our lives. The presence of that Lord is a matter of the functioning of that Spirit in the lives of those who believe, not only in some intellectual assent, but in the total sense of the transformation of life which the Resurrection means for us.

The One Body. Against the background of this reflection on the first Eucharist as the primitive Church remembered it, we can reflect on the meaning of the body of the Lord. And at the outset, trite as it may seem, it is nonetheless important to point out that there is only *one* body of the Lord. And the reason for the importance of this initial observation is the fact that, although we might all agree on this, there is still at least an implicit division on the body of the Lord into a heavenly (real, physical) body and an earthly (mystical, eucharistic) body. And Berengar's problem remains. How can the body of the Lord (i.e., the real physical body) be broken up and scattered all over the altars of the world? His answer was that the Eucharistic body is a "symbol" of the real (i.e., physical) body of the Lord in heaven. But by his time, the symbolic, sacramental consciousness of Christianity had broken down to the extent that "symbolic" and "real" were opposed to each other. Maybe it was the brutal character of the age, when survival was such a consuming concern that focused the attention of the West on the pragmatic and the physical as the realm of the "real." Certainly that aspect of human life demanded a lot of attention and was very "real" for human attention. But in any case the earlier more sacramental consciousness was gone and the real and the symbolic were chasms apart from one another. The grossness of Cardinal Humbert's oath (that the body of the Lord was real and truly broken by the hands of the priest and chewed by the teeth of the faithful) betrays the same literalism and even Alger of Liege's reply that the whole Church is co-present, co-sacramental with the body of the Lord betrays the same literalism when it situates the body *there* on the altar. The villain of the piece is neither exaggerated sacramental realism nor exaggerated sacramental symbolism, but the literalism which underlies both positions, losing sight of the profound symbolic realism which is the heart of the biblical and earlier patristic sacramental vision.

But the oneness of the One body is not a matter of a physical, material and numerical unity—one body among any other number of bodies. The oneness of this body is a oneness which is based on the unique function of this body—the renewal and unification of all creation by God in and under a new Head, Jesus, the Lord. This body, then, is a unique body and this reflection will center on five characteristics which make it unique and give us some understanding of just how different it is from the physical, the literal body. This body is, first of all, a human body. But its human reality is transformed and renewed by the fact that this is a risen body, i.e., a spiritual body, and thus a symbolic or mystical body. Further, it is a body of forgiveness, a body in which man's separation from God, himself and other men is brought healing and unity. And, finally, it is, because of all of this, a eucharistic body, a body of praise, thanksgiving and blessing. Human, risen, symbolic, forgiving, eucharistic—this is the unique oneness and unifying reality of the body of the Lord. And by reflecting on these characteristics of that body, we can come to some appreciation of the new oneness to which God calls us in the body of the Lord.

First, the body is a *human* body. This may seem trite. Jesus is, after all, and always will be human. The hypostatic unity of divine and human in the one Christ is not some sort of melting process in which the divine becomes the human. The council of Chalcedon insists that there is no confusion of the divine and the human, that the difference of the divine and the human is not taken away in this unity but that what is proper to the divine and what is proper to the human remains intact within the unity (DS 302). And for our purposes, this means that the risen Lord is and will forever be human. It is and always will be in and through His human reality that Jesus is one with the Father, one with us, one Lord.

What is important and meaningful for us in this reflection is that the human reality of the body of the Lord speaks in a profoundly new way to *our humanity*. For the literal mind, the literal spirit, it has all been said already—this is all there is, the skin, the bones, the organs, the muscles. This is the human and this is all it will ever be. Once again, the literal spirit is the villain of the piece. But the human body of the Lord tells us that there is a new creation, a new possibility for being human, a new humanity created in God's sight in the holiness and righteousness *if we are to be fully human*. To be skin and bones is not enough. To be geared for action is not enough. Now that the body of the Lord is to be gathered, to grow to its full stature, far more is possible, far more is necessary—and this in order to be human itself. But what is the more, the new? This brings us to the second characteristic of the one body of the Lord.

Second, the one human body of the Lord is a *risen* body, raised from the dead in the Spirit of Holiness (Rom. 1:4). It is a body fashioned to be the organism of a new humanity, a new creation, the imperishable life begun in God's raising Jesus from the dead. And this new life is not a physical life. It is a spiritual life. "It is sown a physical body; it is raised a spiritual body. If there is a physical body, there is also a spiritual body" (I Cor. 15:44). But what does it mean to be a spiritual body? Paul gives us a hint when he states that the last Adam, the new beginning of a new mankind, became a life-giving Spirit. (15:45). This body is brought into being and vivified by the Spirit of the risen Jesus. And when we recall what we mean by "spirit," we can see that this means that this body is constituted by a vision. And the "vision" in question is not just a matter of a seeing eye, although this metaphor is useful for our understanding. This vision is a total vision, the vision of mind and heart, a mind and heart transformed and renewed by the meaning and power of the resurrection of Jesus as this enters our lives and functions there as a living reality. This is a body brought into being by the one Spirit through whom Jesus entered into newness of life as the first-born. It is a body for Jesus, established by God in the one Spirit as the beginning of a new world, a new history. It is a body made up of members whose whole context for living has been transformed and renewed so that they become the organism in which the Living Lord dwells in the world to renew and reunify it. It is a body which lives and functions as the body of the Lord to the extent that we are faithful, true to the very concrete works in which that Spirit enters human lives, manifests its presence, deepens its power for transformation, for renewal of man and history, for the reunification of everything in the Risen Lord.

The body of the Lord is a life-giving Spirit. It is a living, breathing context for our vision, our experience, the whole fabric of our lives. It grafts us into itself by the fruits of that Spirit, as they blossom in the lives of those with whom we share our lives making us members of one another and of the Lord. *But the important thing is that it is a body, a real body—not a physical body, but a spiritual body—but a real body nonetheless.* And it is a body which is constituted by a vision, a body which can only see the world and itself to the extent that new eyes have been opened for it to see—see itself, see the world as newly created by the hand of God. This is what we mean when we say that the body of the Lord is a risen Body.

One can hear the literalist crying out at this point—the literalist in one's self and the literalist in others—what ever happened to the Jesus we knew and loved? Has He been swallowed up, melted down into a community? The answer is "No." He has not been swallowed up or melted down, but the bodily way in which He lives His deeply transformed new human life has been equally deeply transformed. He no longer lives the kind of physical life we live. He lives a spiritual life, a life in which the Spirit in which He is one with the Father is the Spirit which gathers his real, but profoundly changed human body together in the deep transformation of human life which that Spirit means to our lives. Jesus, the Lord, is human, but with a new humanity. He is alive, human, Himself. But all of this is a dazzling new way.

Further, this may sound somewhat like the "christological pantheism" which Heribert Mühlen rightly criticizes. But it is not. For the fact that the body of the Lord is gathered together in the New Spirit does not mean that Jesus Himself disappears in the process. What this could be called is a kind of "christological panentheism," a far different matter. This latter takes the expression of the body of the Lord deeply seriously both for its own sake and for the sake of what this has to say to the reality and possibilities of human life and its destiny. It takes seriously the fact that Jesus personally dwells in His members, the fact that, to the extent that we are faithful to the fruits of His Spirit we are, in living fact, the living, functioning Body of the Lord. And what all this means is that what the body of the Lord means to our concrete human experience can only be seen to be real is we actually live our lives in the fruits of His Spirit—love, joy, peace, patience, kindness, goodness, faithfulness to one another, gentleness and self-control. This is the kind of life which opens in us the eyes with which we can discern the Body of the Lord. It is a risen life brought about in us by the Spirit which possesses us and which we share in sharing its fruits.

Third, from all this it should be apparent what we mean when we say that the one, human risen body of the Lord is a *symbolic,* a *mystical* body. At the risk of being tediously repetitious, we must reiterate that a symbolic body is a real body. But this real body is the body of the Risen Lord. It is that aspect of the human reality of the Lord in which he sees and is seen against the background of the New Creation brought about by God in the reality of the Resurrection. It is that aspect of His human personal reality in which He enters into dialogue with the world and history constantly becoming the Living Lord of an

actual history. And to the extent that the Resurrection, the New
Creation are real, the body which the Lord gathers to Himself
is a real body.

Further this symbolic body is a body of unity. And this
does not mean simply that this is one body. Rather, it means
that the body is one body to the extent that the unity to which
the New Creation calls us is actually brought about in our lives
and history. It is symbolic in the radical sense of *sum-bollein,*
which means a gathering together. And the gathering which
takes place in the body of the Lord is the gathering of men
into the unity of the New Creation in the one Spirit. This means
that this body is created by a vision, the vision which sees man
and history renewed and summoned to be constantly renewed
in the kind of unity which comes into being as the fruits of that
Spirit really function in our lives. Thus, the gift which we are
called to be to each other in the unfailing constancy of love to
which we are called, is a gift of Spirit, a gift of vision through
which the Spirit bears witness within our spirit that God has in
fact raised Jesus from the dead and that that new life can be
ours not only in the life after death but in the reality of our
lives here and now. This vision, this spirit is the pledge of the
imperishable life which is God's promise. Through this vision,
in this Spirit, all the world, all our lives are called to be
gathered into a new unity. Thus, the capacity to see this body,
the capacity to be seen as this body, is a matter of the gift and
sharing of the seeing eye of grace, the grace which transforms
our consciousness, our freedom, our hopes into a new spirit.
The symbolic body can only be seen through the eyes of the
new Spirit, through the eyes of a mystical vision which goes
beyond the physical to see the power and reality of the spiritual.
Through this vision all of man's world and all of his history
can be seen to be the sacrament of the faithful love and the
saving promise of our God. It is all a matter of developing the
eyes to see. The vision makes us into the body of the Lord.

There is another reflection which should be important for
our understanding of the symbolic reality of the one human

body of the Lord. This is the fact that this is the body *of the Lord*. This means that it is not only a matter of *our* capacity to be and see all that the body of the Lord means in terms of renewal, unity and the transformation of the whole fabric of human life and history, but that is also a matter of the Lord's capacity to be and see this newness of creation. In other words, Jesus can only see Himself as real and living Lord to the extent that the transformation of everything which His being Lord means is in fact taking place. Jesus needs His body to be Lord, to see and act in the world as Lord. The Lord cannot be Lord without His Body, without the gathering, without the new vision coming into being. It may seem redundant to point out that the Lord cannot be Lord until He is in fact Lord, but this is very important for our understanding of and attitude toward God. We can treat the reality of God in a frozen and distant way, as a reality which does not need us to be itself, a reality which need not care about us for its own reality. But from this perspective we can see that what being God means concretely and historically is very much a matter of what takes place in our lives. And from this perspective we can see that the gift of sharing in the life of the Trinity is not an abstract or neutral fact. We really do share in that life; we have a real part and function in Jesus' becoming Lord, in God's becoming God: all in all. The sharing in the one Spirit really does mean a sharing in the life, the concrete historical life of God.

Fourth, the body of the Lord—the one, human risen symbolic body—is a *body of forgiveness*. For the experience which gives this body its vision and gathers it into its unique oneness is the experience of forgiveness. In our reflection on the New Creation, we went into what the experience of forgiveness should be. The new creation, the new humanity transformed by the Spirit of the Lord is a forgiven creation, a forgiven humanity. It is forgiveness which gives the body of the Lord the eyes to see itself and everything else as transformed, renewed in a great new act of God. In terms of this reflection, we can characterize the experience of forgiveness as a new experience of *unity*. We know that the reality of the Resurrection calls us to a new human unity in the body of the Lord and that the full maturity of that body consists in a new unity is a oneness which must be brought about in the one Spirit in the midst of a deeply divided humanity. What needs forgiving is the division, the separation of man from man, of man from himself, of man from God within this deep human division.

But this healing, forgiving unity is a reality which comes about in our lives in the one Spirit. It is only to the extent that this Spirit takes over more and more of our lives and brings its fruits to blossom there that we are really forgiven in any real and functioning way. And maybe more than anything else, the experience of this forgiveness is the experience of a new and hope-filled unity with ourselves, with one another and in all of this with God. It is the experience of the healing of a division, but it is important to know what this division is and why it is in us and between us. Let us begin within ourselves.

Religion, like any other human activity, can be geared for action or geared for union. We are all familiar with religion geared for action. The action, all too often, is the action of dividing, dividing body from spirit, concentrating on the life of spirit and more or less hoping that body will go away. We create an ideal image of the ideal religious person, all serene and without passion, eyes on heavenly things and turned ever away from the sordid affairs of earth, body, the human in a fervent search for union with the divine by separation from everything else. Of course, this is not unique to religion. It also happens to people who just plain hate themselves for some less noble reason. There is no value, no goodness or worth in the person we actually are. So we put our hope in being someone else, some kind of ideal self we had far rather be. We find values outside ourselves and hang all our hopes on them. We put all our energy into being rich, sexy, powerful—or "virtuous." We are, in a word, divided off from part or even all of ourselves and put all our hopes in that phantom ideal which we pursue with all our resources. We have to be somebody, but since what we are is nobody and nowhere, we split off from that and try to set up a self which is more acceptable—to ourselves. Religious or not, this kind of division cuts us off from the place where alone there is hope that the fundamental principle of any worth might begin to operate effectively in our lives. That place is the place in which we come to accept the incredible fact that we are loved and that therefore eminently lovable, worthwhile, good. This kind of division divides us off from the basic reality of grace, namely that *before* we achieve anything, *before* we do nice things, we are loved, radically and totally loved. So, in the absence of this kind of faith, we must struggle with might and main to make ourselves lovable by putting on a good show. And show it is since it doesn't reflect anything real in our lives. Once again, it may be "religious" or it may be just plain sick, but the effect is the same: the crippling division from ourselves which condemns us to the terrible punishment of constantly trying to please ourselves.

If the division wreaks this kind of havoc on our own personal life, it is equally, if not more disastrous for our relations with the people with whom we live. Either we spend our time defending ourselves from the terrible event of someone actually seeing what is behind our performance, the horrible possibility that someone will get behind the mask. We cut our lives off from those around us for self-protection or else we treat everyone else as we treat ourselves, as people whose lives are to be managed and manipulated like our own, pawns in our own search for power, wealth or "virtue."

The important point in all this (and it is far from a complete analysis) is that the division from ourselves and the division and the division from others is at the same time a division from the only thing that can give us any worth, the only thing that can free us from the rat-race to which we condemn ourselves— and that one thing is the unqualified, absolutely faithful love of God—a love without demand, without condition in terms of our "performance." This is a love which is always "before," preceding any effort we might make to "please God." We might call such vain efforts an attempt to "please God," but they are in fact usually attempts to please ourselves, to give ourselves some kind of worth. By some ineluctable logic the division from ourselves seems to lead relentlessly to the division from others, to division from God. We end up manipulating others for the sake of our own worth and we serve an idol created out of our own profound need. The presence, the past and the future of an illusion. *This* is *not* my body; something else, someone else, *that* is my body.

What is there which can heal this division, forgive and overcome this separation? Once again, it is a matter of Spirit. It is a matter of the transformation of the vision, the whole context out of which we live. It is a matter of our having the eyes to see in a total and transforming way that we are in fact loved, lovable, valuable, worthwhile. And for this to happen, it is not enough for us to sit and say over and over to ourselves, "I *am* worthwhile. I *am* . . ." That would only be replacing one illusion with another. What is needed is a whole new spirit, a whole new real and functioning context for our vision, our experience, the pattern of our lives. And that spirit is the Spirit manifested and at work in the fruits which the Spirit of the Lord produce in human lives: love, joy, peace, patience, kindness, goodness, faithfulness to one another, gentleness and self-control. The life which is made up of the sharing of these fruits creates a profound change of vision, a profound change of spirit. This kind of life frees us from the fact and the penalty of the division into which we have fallen. It frees us over and over again from the fear, the dreadful performance which seeks to make a spirit of dread and despair. This kind of life renews us, renews the earth, calling us to life, real life, our very own life. It is only in and out of this Spirit that we can look at the whole of ourselves, the who of our lives and say with praise and thanksgiving to God, "Yes! This *is* my body!" And with this confession the transsubstantiation can take place, the liberation of a whole new capacity to live. Only in the fruits of this Spirit can we "get it together" again. Only in this Spirit can we see that we are indeed the Body of the Lord living in a transformed world, a new creation.

This, then, is the one body of the Lord—human, risen, symbolic, forgiving—a unique body for the Lord of the New Creation. And perhaps in the light of this last consideration, we can see that the experience, the concrete meaning of the body of the Lord comes into function and into our vision most clearly in the healing of division which is the occasion and the terminus of our fallenness. It is out of this experience more than any other that the "body of the Lord" can mean something real, something functioning powerfully in human life and experience. For when this is an actual fact than in truth "all have been baptized into one body in one Spirit and all have drunk of one Spirit" (I Cor. 12:13).

From all this, then, we can begin to appreciate the fact that the one body of the Lord is a *eucharistic* body, a body whose voice is a voice of praise and blessing to God for the newness of life which He has brought into being in raising Jesus from the dead and in seeding our lives with the promise for our lives which the living Spirit is and will be. It is in the fruits which that Spirit bears in the daily pattern of our lives which erupts spontaneously into praise and blessing for the unfailing love with which God has renewed the earth. Eucharist is no longer simply performance, a ritual to please God who is angry at us. Eucharist springs from our lips and hearts because we know that the love of God is true, is faithful, that it will not fail because His Spirit pledges us faithfully to one another in the works of love and faithfulness to one another, no matter what. Eucharist is a celebration, a celebration of the reality, the living, functioning, transforming, healing reality of the one Body of the Risen Lord.

Conclusion: It's all a matter of Spirit. It is the Spirit of the Lord which gathers the body of the Lord into its unique and marvelous oneness. But a very sobering thought remains. When we reflect on the meaning of our being the Body of the Lord and then look at our lives as they actually are, a disturbing question cannot but rise in our minds. How can we dare to celebrate Eucharist when in fact our lives are far from the unity of the body of the Lord? Are we celebrating this sacrament in Spirit, in truth? This is a sobering question indeed and it is a question which should be a part of every Eucharist. Paul assailed the spirit of the community of Corinth, telling them that theirs was not the Lord's supper because they could not really discern the body. And their lack of discernment was obvious in the judgment which God leveled against their community in the very earthly and human terms of the neglect of the poor and the weak in their own midst. Every time they ate the bread and drank the cup they ate and drank this judgment. Instead of eating the bread of life, they were eating the bitter bread of their own division, of their own lack of the Spirit of the Lord. The same is true of us. Our Eucharist should have a bitter taste indeed if we are divided from ourselves, from one another—as in fact we are. The scandal of this division eats at the very heart of our eucharist and vitiates its sacramental power.

The aim of these reflections has been to come to some appreciation of the importance of the Spirit—not only for a meaningful theology of sacrament, but for the possibility of filling our sacramental life with the living experiential meaning they should have. The aim of these reflections has been to attempt to show what that Spirit is and how it should function in our lives. Maybe, if we can see this, we might begin to make some efforts at a real renewal of Christian life, of Christian sacraments. For renewal is not just a matter of the reformation of the symbol system. It is rather the renewal in our lives and experience of the living content of the symbol systems, the structure, the ritual, the language. And this can only happen when the experience which gave rise to these symbol systems becomes our experience. It can only happen when the transformation of vision and life which took place at the resurrection of Jesus and gave men eyes to see that Jesus is risen, that He is Lord, takes place in our vision, our lives.

Thus, the question for our sacramental life is not "Is he there?" but "Is it true?" Is what we profess in this celebration of the one body of the risen Lord—is this true in our lives? For it is in this truth that there lives the power of this sacrament to constantly renew our lives.

Send forth your Spirit and they shall be called to life
And you will renew the face of the earth.

[Ps 103]